# CONTROL THE CRAZY

# VINNY GUADAGNINO
# CONTROL THE CRAZY

## My Plan to Stop Stressing, Avoid Drama, and Maintain Inner Cool

with Samantha Rose

THREE RIVERS PRESS

NEW YORK

This book is Vinny's story about how he personally manages his general anxiety disorder. It is not meant to dispense medical advice or prescribe the use of any technique as a form of treatment for anxiety disorders or similar conditions. Each individual dealing with emotional health issues such as anxiety or depression may experience different symptoms and may benefit from potential treatment approaches such as lifestyle changes, talk therapy, and/or medication. We strongly recommend that you consult with your doctor about questions and concerns specific to your health. The authors and publisher expressly disclaim responsibility for any adverse effects that may result from the use or application of the information contained in this book.

Three Rivers Press and the Tugboat design are registered trademarks of Random House, Inc.

Originally published in hardcover in the United States by Crown Archetype, an imprint of the Crown Publishing Group, a division of Random House, Inc., New York, in 2012.

Library of Congress Cataloging-in-Publication Data is available upon request.

ISBN 978-0-307-98726-6
eISBN 978-0-307-98725-9

Printed in the United States of America

Book design by Ralph Fowler/RLF Design
Cover design by Michael Nagin
Cover photography © Robert Trachtenberg

10  9  8  7  6  5  4  3  2  1

First Paperback Edition

To all my teachers who have inspired me,
and to friends and family who've helped me along.

Thank you for sharing this message with me.
I hope to do you proud.

# CONTENTS

# INTRODUCTION: Have You Heard?

I'm best known as the "peacekeeper," the "voice of reason," and the most "level-headed, drama-free" guido on MTV's *Jersey Shore,* yet there's more to Vinny G than meets the eye.

What most people don't know about me—including, until recently, not even my own mother—is that my head is not often *that* level. The truth is, I suffer from chronic anxiety. I can work myself up into a fearful, paralyzing state of mind that can last for days, weeks, and even *months* where I feel mad scared, totally isolated and alone, overwhelmed, and completely out of control. Imagine being stuck in a bad dream you can't wake up from. This is how I often feel—except it's not a dream, but the relentless voice in my own head I can't shake.

There have been many times in my life when my anxious mind has spun so out of control that I've simply had to bail. Packing my bags and walking off the set of *Jersey Shore* is one example. Leaving college is another. I'm talking anxiety that causes night sweats, insomnia, extreme weight loss, headaches, and a mind that won't shut the 'eff up! For real, I can get *low,* and when I'm in my low-down dark and scary place, I feel crazy.

It turns out that the *real* Vinny Guadagnino has a pretty serious condition—generalized anxiety disorder. I share my struggle with more than forty million people in the United States alone who are living with some sort of anxiety disorder. But what separates me from most adults and teens who suffer from anxiety, stress, and feeling overwhelmed with what life is throwing them is that I've spent the past three years taking charge of my mental challenge by developing a step-by-step program that not only has helped me get a handle on my anxious mind but has also filled me with a sense of personal power and control that has rocked every area of my life, from building a dream team of friends and colleagues to meeting super cool girls, getting in the best physical shape I've ever been in, and landing awesome career opportunities.

Sounds good, right? You want a piece of the action? If you can relate to the kind of "crazy" mind I'm describing here, you picked up the right book. Or if you're someone who only occasionally feels low, what I offer in the pages ahead can help you, too.

Check it: the book you hold in your hands isn't just for people who struggle with a generalized anxiety disorder like I do. You don't have to have something "serious" or diagnosable to learn a few tricks from me. Having a mind that sometimes takes a run on you is more normal than you might think. The truth is that from time to time, most people let their thoughts get them down and allow their emotions to stand in their way. The program I developed is for anyone who gets generally stressed, nervous, frustrated, pissed off, sad, and occasionally feels knocked around by life. (I can't speak for you, but that about covers everyone *I* know.) Work pressure, family conflict, financial baggage, relationship drama, academic trouble, poor body image, and low self-esteem—on any given day these challenges can get the best of us. Any and all of them can make us feel crazy.

When I was at my lowest point, I had a hard time finding the right book to help me control *my* crazy, one that spoke to me on my level. Much of the self-help mumbo jumbo on the shelves, books you'd find in a doctor's office with titles like *It's Gonna Get Worse Before It Gets Better,* left me feeling more messed up and confused than I had before I opened the cover. I felt the doctor, expert, professor, or whoever didn't understand *my* experience or really get where I was coming from.

That's when I started reading a *different* type of book—titles that were more "spiritual" in nature (as in written by hard-core Buddhist monks, not psychologists); and I'm not kidding—as soon as I started reading them, my life began to change. The more I learned about the mind-body-spirit "triple-threat" approach to mental health, the better I felt and the faster I regained control of my life. Then it hit me. What if I tried to fill the void? Since I hadn't easily found the right motivational message to guide me when I needed it most, others who were suffering might be coming up empty too. Maybe there was a way I could pass on what I'd learned in one easy-to-read guidebook, one that kids and adults I knew could relate to and understand.

*Control the Crazy* is my no-bullshit program for doing just that—getting a handle on the everyday challenges that mentally, physically, and spiritually trip us up. It includes my adaptation and translation of many key teachings and techniques by some of the most popular and influential spiritual teachers, philosophers, and masters in the field of personal growth today. To keep it interesting, I've included my own stories, insights, and mental workouts for kicking anxiety's ass and overcoming everyday high-stress situations.

My program is specifically designed so you can apply it to your own life, whoever you are. You see, *Control the Crazy* doesn't dwell so much on *what* stresses you out or what you struggle with. No matter. We've all got something. What's most important is that whatever's got you down, you have a set of simple, kick-ass tools that you can pull out of your back pocket and put to use right away.

*Control the Crazy* will specifically help you:

- Deal with drama and life's little annoyances without "losing" it

- Manage haters, bullies, and negative people in your life

- Bounce back from benders, binges, and hangovers

- Boost your confidence so you kill it at work or in school

- Give you focus and mad game with the opposite sex

- Develop stronger relationships with your peeps

- Maintain your inner cool when you're on the verge of feeling "crazy"

How does it work? When I went looking for the tools to beat back my anxiety and my low-down, dark and scary moods, I discovered that if I could simply master my mind, I could control my bad days rather than let them control me. Whether you realize it or not, it's the critical and self-defeating voice in your own head that often spins a crappy situation to a whole new level of crazy. Said a different way—you've got the power. *You can handle anything and anyone when you simply change how you think.*

Maybe you're wondering—What gives Vinny Guadagnino of *Jersey Shore*—a show famous for fist pumping, hooking up, and delivering at least one good punch in the face in every episode—the credibility to write a book like this? I mean, who do I think I am? How can I be taken seriously?

Believe me, I've heard it all before. I've read blogs that are "shocked" I even know how to put a sentence together. If you're confused by what you thought I was all about and what you're reading here, let me clear something up for you—yes, I like to party, and I also have a brain. Not only that, I've got the best credibility of all: *I've been there and I've come out on the other side.* It's true, I'm not a shrink or a doctor, an expert, or a priest. I'm just a twenty-four-year-old kid who's made a name for himself on a reality TV show. In many ways, my life and career are just getting started. Still, I've been through a lot for my age, so what I *do* have is life experience. I get it on a personal level. I've struggled. I *still* struggle, and I've discovered that there's a way to get through it. I want you to know you aren't alone.

You see—it doesn't matter who you are—life is hard. Every day, I meet kids and adults, either at the club, on set, or in my favorite barbershop on Staten Island, who are stressed out, unhappy, and caught up in their own negative drama and who I think could benefit from the same tools that have helped me.

While I may be most recognized for my T-shirts, tattoos, and manicured eyebrows, I believe that the most important role you can play in life is to be of service to other people. I know—*awww, shucks*—but it's the truth. Nothing makes me happier and gives me a sense of purpose more than helping people who need a hand. Sure, the "me-me-me" celebrity lifestyle is a rush, I'm not gonna lie. But fame and a loaded bank account don't mean a thing if you're suffering. I know better than anyone that you can't enjoy the good life if you're operating from a dark place. I've struggled with anxiety for most of my young adult life, and I consider myself extremely blessed that whenever life trips me up and I stumble and fall, I have the tools in my back pocket to pick myself back up.

Now it's your turn. Is life getting you down? Do *you* need a hand? Then take mine and let me help you.

# PART ONE
# MY JOURNEY

# THE STORY BEHIND THE STORY

You may have seen me recently and very publicly hit my emotional "breaking point" during season 5 of *Jersey Shore*. I bailed from the Seaside house, setting off rumors that I may have left the show for good. Yet, regardless of what you've seen on TV or read, trust me when I say—*no one knows the story I'm about to share with you.*

To fully understand my behavior, it's important you know what led up to it. So, let's go back several years to when this story really began.

\* \* \*

It was 2009. I was a twenty-two-year-old kid, living the life—partying in Seaside Heights, sharing a coed beach house with seven tanned and toned guidos and guidettes, and hooking up with super hot girls on a national TV show. Yet, two weeks into the filming of the premiere season of *Jersey Shore*—BOOM!—I awoke one night out of a dead sleep short of breath. I couldn't get enough air; I felt like I was friggin' suffocating. My heart began to race, and I was seized by feelings of dread and doom. I was having an anxiety attack.

*I'm trapped. I have to get out of here.*

All my roommates were nervous to some degree. On a reality TV set, cameras follow you around day and night, and it's no surprise their constant 24/7 presence can create some stress. But that's not what was bothering me. The dark, oppressive cloud that was closing in around me had nothing to do with cameras, crews, or craft services. Rather it had everything to do with what was going on *inside* me.

Thankfully, I'd scored one of the few single rooms in the house, so when the attack hit I was removed from my seven roommates. They had no clue that I was wide awake, pacing the floors and freaking out. I spent most of the late-night hours feeling trapped in my single bedroom, convinced I was losing it and my head was going to burst. My mind was spinning on high speed, as if my thoughts had been thrown into an industrial-strength washing machine.

On a reality TV set, you're basically cut off from the sounds of the outside world—no phone, Internet, TV, or radio. Besides the noise *we* make, it's relatively quiet. When I'm at home on Staten Island, I usually fall asleep with the TV on, but when I'm shooting *Jersey Shore* there's nothing like that to distract me from my thoughts. And trust me, the crazy, doomsday thoughts I was having that night were not the kind you want to be left alone in bed with.

Because I'd been picked for the show to fill the role of the authentic and fun-loving guido who liked to fist-pump on camera, I was afraid to tell anyone about what was going on in my head. Being on the show was a huge opportunity, and I didn't want to blow it. So for the next several days I tried to ignore my anxiety, push through, and fake it for the cameras. I pretended I was having a good time, but the truth was that I felt disconnected and alone. Every minute of every hour, I felt like an outcast standing outside a house party watching everyone inside having fun. I went through the motions, playing the class clown, but my mind was in a dark place. I feared that the fun-loving Vinny that the MTV producers were counting on had disappeared. If I didn't quickly snap out of my funk during the brief six weeks we were filming, I was going to come off looking like a major head case on national TV. Problem was—I'd been in this low-down place before, and that hell ride had lasted several months. *What was I going to do?* The world was watching. I was on a locked set. This was the worst possible scenario for someone like me—someone who suffers from chronic anxiety.

*   *   *

My battle with anxiety first reared its ugly head when I was a freshman in high school. I'd always been a pretty likable and funny kid, though I had my share of insecurities that sometimes tripped me up. For example, in the looks department, I battled with pimples, braces, and a mess of thick hair that made me look like a white Fresh Prince of Bel-Air. My hair looked, and felt, like a friggin' Brillo pad. Add to that, my family never had a lot of money, so I was always struggling to "fit" the part. I definitely didn't have the freshest sneakers. I certainly didn't drive the nicest car. And to top it off, I tried out for the high school basketball team my freshman year but didn't make it unless you count benchwarmer as a position. I was bullied by the popular jocks, and girls weren't all that interested in talking to me. I always felt a little bit awkward, like I was on the outside of life, you know? Regardless, I had a group of friends who seemed to think I was pretty cool, so all in all, I considered myself pretty normal.

Until . . .

One day, I was sitting in English class when from out of nowhere my heart started pounding, my vision went blurry, I became dizzy and light headed, and my teacher's voice sounded muddled and distorted. It was like what Charlie Brown hears whenever a grown-up is speaking to him: "Whaa-whaa-whaa." I was paralyzed; the classroom walls felt like they were closing in around me, and I was physically unable to move. I had no idea what was happening, and I certainly wasn't going to tell the gangster Spanish kid with the neck tattoo sitting behind me, "Hey, I think I'm having a heart attack. Call an ambulance." He would've definitely looked at me like I had ten heads. So I just sat still for what felt like *forever* and prayed for the feeling to pass. The entire episode probably only lasted for twenty seconds, but it felt like a lifetime. *What the hell was that?* I couldn't think of anything specific that would have caused me to freak out like that. It was just an ordinary day in English class.

I didn't have a name for it at the time, but I later came to understand that I'd suffered my first anxiety attack. After that, similar attacks became somewhat regular. Since they didn't seem to be triggered by anything specific, I lived in constant fear of being hit with one. Just knowing that it *might* happen was sometimes all it would take to set one in motion. My heart would start pounding, I'd begin to sweat, and my head would go into spin mode. I'd grip the sides of my school desk, afraid to move, speak, or breathe until my anxiety passed.

I was sure I was the only fourteen-year-old in the world who suffered like this, so I was embarrassed to tell anyone what was going on. I didn't want my friends to think I was weird or to worry any-one—my mom, especially—so I learned how to wait out the attacks. It worked. By my senior year at Susan E. Wagner High School on Staten Island, my anxiety had almost completely disappeared. In fact, I'd nearly forgotten about it until my first year of college, when the attacks returned with renewed force, knocking me into my first deep depression.

## HOLD UP

## Too Much, Too Soon

If you're thinking, *Vinny's a mess! I can't relate to this guy. He slips into dark places I've never fallen into*—hold on right there. While the dark holes I've crawled out of have been very dark indeed, you don't have to be someone who suffers from anxiety, depression, or anything "diagnosable" to benefit from this book. The tools I roll out for you in the chapters ahead can be used to manage any stressful situation, tough ordeal, or unexpected dark day. For sure, you can relate to that, right?

# WHAT THE FUNK?

I was seventeen when I started college at the State University of New York (SUNY) at New Paltz. I was young, and to be honest, I was a little nervous to leave the mother's nest on Staten Island, but I was also excited to party and study away at college. I'd gotten a pretty sweet scholarship thanks to my high grade point average in high school and extracurricular activities outside of school. Also, I'd written a pretty dope college essay about growing up in a full-on Italian family that started with: "So, I'm eating meatballs with my Uncle Nino . . ." I was nervy for sure, but felt ready to jump into the college experience one hundred percent. And I was sure I was prepared for it.

On a late-summer day, my mother, my father, my big sister, my cousins, and my aunt helped me move into the dorm. No joke, I was the only kid moving into college who brought nearly ten relatives along for the ride. It took a caravan of three cars to transport all of us and all of my stuff to the school. As soon as we arrived, Mom began hauling in boxes of homemade bread, chicken cutlets, meatballs, and marinara sauce, along with Easy Mac, Devil Dogs, Yodels, and enough potato chips to feed everyone on my floor. I could have easily run a high-class moneymaking food ring out of my dorm room, and in fact, it soon gained a reputation as the place to go when the cafeteria was closed. In addition to all the food, Mom made sure to bring along a year's worth of cleaning supplies, an industrial-strength floor fan, and a fire extinguisher that she insisted I mount on the wall "just in case." Mom—*really*?

If you've seen my mother, Paola, in any of her cameo appearances on *Jersey Shore,* you know that what I'm describing is absolutely true to her character. She's the nurturing, loving mother who lives for taking care of people. She's not just my mom—she's *everybody's* mom.

I'd moved into a triple room with two other guys—one who arrived with a single backpack and the other whose big-ticket item was a TV. Both of my new roommates watched my crazy Italian family fussing all over me and were totally amused, and it didn't take long before my mom took both my roomies in like they were her own. After several hours of getting me settled and situated, my aunt and cousin had to physically remove my mother from my dorm room. She was all tears. "Ma," I told her, "I'm only going to be an hour and a half away." This was no consolation; her baby boy was leaving the nest. Yes, the tabloids have labeled me right—I *am* a mama's boy.

She waved a sad good-bye like on some after-school special about a son going off to college. It was a long, drawn-out farewell, and *finally* they drove off, leaving me to start a new life at SUNY.

That night, I went to my first college frat party. It was exactly how I imagined it would be: kegs of beer, drunken sorority girls doing SoCo and lime shots, frat guys playing beer pong and flip cup, and

Shaggy's "It Wasn't Me" blasting in the background. I hung with my new crew—a mix of guys from Staten Island, Long Island, Queens, and the Bronx that I'd met on my dorm floor. *I finally made it out of my house, and I'm in for a wild ride,* I thought. The party scene was poppin', and as far as school was concerned, I was mad psyched about kicking ass in all my classes.

But not even a month into my first semester, I started to notice that feeling of anxiety creeping back into my life. Every day, I became a little bit more nervous and tense. The drastic difference between my old home life and my new dorm life was definitely affecting me. My privacy was gone, my ability to focus was jacked, and sharing a room with two other guys made it hard for me to sleep at night. I would toss and turn, get out of bed and do push-ups, watch TV, sometimes wander the hallways. Eventually this turned into full-blown insomnia, and my anxiety became chronic.

Yet when I thought about it on a rational level, life wasn't that stressful, was it? Did I really have a legit reason to feel so messed up? I'd gotten into a great college. I was living on my own in a coed dorm. I was killing it in school, and to top it all off, I'd recently lost my virginity to one of the hot sorority girls on the floor directly above me. I was living the college dream! Life was great, right? *Then why,* I wondered, *do I feel like shit?*

There were parties to go to, new people to meet, but all I wanted to do was catch up on my sleep and escape the constant stream of nagging thoughts in my head. I'd lie awake at night, consumed with thoughts about the pointlessness of life, like *Why am I even here? What's my purpose? What's the reason for my being alive?* It would not stop. I felt like I was going crazy. Imagine some demon-possessed merry-go-round in a horror flick—that was my mind. No matter how hard I tried, I couldn't get off the ride. And when I wasn't consumed by my thoughts, I was obsessed with getting physically sick. I'd become a mad hypochondriac. No doubt about it, I was a mess.

Convinced that I was a real freak show—that my anxiety was unique to me and that I belonged in the psych ward—I started to withdraw from everyone around me. I stopped hanging out with my roommates and my campus crew; I couldn't relate to them anymore. Actually, it was the other way around. I worried that they wouldn't relate to *me*. If they knew what was going on in my head, they'd think I was a nut job, for sure. Yet oddly enough, no one seemed to notice that anything was wrong. While I thought it was totally obvious I was falling apart, what I quickly discovered was that on the outside, I appeared pretty together. I could still carry on a conversation, laugh at people's jokes, smile at girls across campus, and sit in class like a regular guy. Still, I knew something was off—*way off*—and preferred to stay holed up in my dorm room when I wasn't in class. I'd pace the floors like a friggin' mouse trapped in a cage with a mind that was going in a million directions. By the time the weekend would roll around, I'd be on the phone with Mom, begging her to come and get me. My mom's an overly protective Italian mother, so as soon as she heard the slightest sadness in my voice, without even questioning the cause of it, she'd hop in the car and drive an hour and a half out of her way—and in the *snow,* no less—to fetch her "baby." As soon as I'd get home to Staten Island, I'd lock myself in my bedroom, curl up in a ball on my bed, and pray that my screaming head would stop.

This went on for months, until my anxiety eventually spiraled so out of control that I stopped fighting it. I was sure my life couldn't get any worse, and it wasn't going to get any better. I actually began considering putting myself out of my misery by committing suicide. For real, my mind *went there.* A cousin of mine had killed himself when he was in his early twenties, and I wondered, *Is this how he felt right before he took his life? Is suicide where I'm headed too?* My head started to fill with images of me hanging from a rope in a basement. I realize now that I didn't want to die, but I was desperately afraid that the pain I was feeling would last forever.

One night when the noise in my head got too crazy for me to handle, I stormed out of my dorm room and into the night. Feeling totally isolated and scared, I walked around the dimly lit campus yelling at God. I was raised in the Catholic Church and had always prayed to an external God—some guy with a white beard floating around in the clouds. I screamed at God, "Why are you letting this happen? Why are you making me suffer? I've always been a good kid, and *this* is what you're doing for me? Are you kidding?" I was taught, and believed, that in man's greatest time of need, God will be there to comfort and keep you safe. So where was my God now? I felt like I'd been abandoned. Was I cursed? At my lowest point, I played the only card left in my deck: I abruptly left college in the middle of the semester and returned home.

When friends and family asked why I'd left school, I chalked it up to being homesick. I told them that I'd had a tough time adjusting to college life and needed "a break." And a part of me really *hoped* that by simply moving home and seeing my family again on a regular basis, I'd be able to crawl out of my dark place. But changing my address didn't change anything. My anxiety was coming from inside me. It followed me everywhere I went, even home to the house where I grew up.

Over the Christmas and New Year's holidays, this truth hit me hard. The Guadagnino household is nuts (in the good way) over the holidays, and it's always been my favorite time of year. Imagine eighty, or what feels like eighty, Italians packed into a small kitchen and dining room with trays of homemade food on the stove, in the oven, and spread out all over the countertops. My mother and my aunts rule the kitchen—cooking, gossiping, and poking fun at everyone in their path—while my wild Uncle Nino typically takes center stage in the dining room with a bottle of wine and tells his dirtiest jokes. This gets Uncle Sal, our resident Godfather, riled up. He'll join in with some inappropriate sound effect, like a burp or a fart, that might incite the disapproval of my grandmother, who likes to smack people with shoes. Uncle Angelo, the pretty boy and the favorite (seriously, no one gets more girls than Angelo), will crack up at this, and before you know it, kids start screaming and running around, everyone's doubled over, clinking glasses and roaring with laughter. No joke, the noise level in our house can sound like you're in a football stadium.

Family time like this is what I live for. Whether it be Sunday dinner, someone's birthday party, a baby shower, or holiday madness, these parties have always made me happier than anything else in the world. Yet the year I left school, I couldn't connect to that happy feeling. Where I'd usually be right in the middle of it all, egging my uncles on and jumping into all the fun-loving insanity, that year I felt like I didn't belong. I remember sitting at the dinner table surrounded by my aunts and sisters, feeling totally alone. There was love and laughter all around me, and I just sat there, all quiet and detached. No matter how hard I tried, I couldn't get out of my crazy head and relate to the world around me. Imagine one of those slo-mo scenes in an indie film where the camera zooms in on the main character while everything around him is thrown out of focus.

The fact that I felt disconnected from my own family didn't make any sense to me. It actually terrified me! What happened to the kid who always felt safe at home? *Where's Vinny?* I seriously didn't know who I was anymore. How could I feel this lost in the house I'd lived in my whole life, surrounded by the people who love me most? *What the hell!* I thought, *If I can't feel safe here, I'm not safe anywhere.* I tried so hard to fight through it, but the dark and anxious feeling I had in my chest just wouldn't go away.

My mom could tell that I wasn't quite right. She called it a "funk," but she had no idea how bad I felt, and she also didn't ask a lot of questions. I wanted to open up to her and explain that what I was feeling was much *funkier* than she even knew, but I held back. I love my mom, and we're close, but there are certain things I can't say to her, like *Ma, I'm scared. I feel alone and totally separate from everyone and everything around me, like I'm floating in outer space with no lifeline back to the mother ship.* Plus I was confused. I really couldn't put into words what was going on with me. I didn't understand me either! All I knew for sure was that I felt crazy—and this is a hard thing to tell your mother. I didn't want to burden her, or scare her, so in an effort to protect her, I kept my struggle to myself. For nearly a month I stayed in my room, stretched out on my king-size bed with my English bulldog, Jelly, snoring and farting on the floor.

Determined to feel better, I forced myself one afternoon to go to church. It was the first time I'd gone to Confession in years, and I unloaded about my feelings of loss and abandonment. I told the priest, "I think I've hit rock bottom, and I don't know what to do." He suggested I pray, and yet I *had* been praying! I'd been downright begging God to help me feel better, and my desperate pleas were getting me nowhere. I left church feeling frustrated, and determined to find a solution.

# BACK IN THE RING

One day in church, I turned to my godmother, Aunt Mariann, and asked her for advice. Now understand this, my aunt Mariann is a real hard-ass; she calls it like she sees it. There's no bullshitting her. On that particular day in church, I told her I was feeling really messed up. She too had noticed that I wasn't the "same ole Vin," and when I opened up to her about my wild, "crazy" mind, she leveled with me. She said, "Vin, honey—enough. You need to go talk to someone. You need to let it all out."

I thought to myself, *Is she telling me to see a shrink?* Look, I'm a proud, stubborn Italian man. If I can generalize for a moment here, Italian men don't need therapists. If you've got a problem, you suck it up! In the Italian culture, seeking mental help from a doctor is weak and, not only that, it's embarrassing. I'm sure you're familiar with the HBO series *The Sopranos*. There was nothing more shameful for a mob boss than to cry on a therapist's couch. And yet, when my aunt suggested I seek professional help, I knew she was right.

We randomly selected a therapist off my mom's insurance list, and the next thing I knew, I was sitting across the room from my first head doctor. I told this woman about all my panicky and anxious thoughts, about the obsessive questions about existence that plagued me night and day. I explained that I felt crazy, that my thoughts had me trapped in a dark hole, and I worried that I'd never get myself out. After listening to me bitch and whine on and on about how scared, helpless, and abnormal I felt, she reassured me what I was going through was not that uncommon. In fact, she said, my behavior was pretty normal.

*What the . . . ?*

She explained that everyone gets overwhelmed, worked up, and stressed. For some people like myself, when our stress levels hit the roof, our minds go into hyper-drive and we become extremely anxious. I learned that anxiety is a very normal reaction to all kinds of stress and that for some people, it can spin out of control, messing with your life, your relationships, your job performance, and your overall sense of confidence and self-esteem. Anxieties come in all shapes and sizes, and collectively they affect tens of millions of Americans, including a very high percentage of adolescents and teens.

Hearing this made me feel a little more normal again, like I wasn't alone and that no matter how weird my thoughts, they were actually within the parameters of what other people thought sometimes. *Who would've guessed?* For as long as I could remember, I'd convinced myself that I was the only freak show in town. I wondered, how many other kids back at school were suffering in silence, afraid of being labeled weird or crazy? It finally made sense to me why so many kids consider suicide. If you feel totally alone, like no one understands or "gets" you, you become desperate for a way out.

## You're Stronger Than You Think

If you're reading this and thinking, *I know that anxious feeling. I've been there!* or *I am there*, please know you're not alone. There's nothing shameful about what you're going through. Feeling dark, depressed, anxious, worried, or stressed over work, school, a relationship, moving to a new city, whatever, is more normal than you know, and asking for help is not a sign of weakness; rather, it's a sign of strength.

As it sometimes can do, *my* anxiety had spiraled into a deep depression, so my therapist suggested antidepressant medication. My experience with recreational drugs was that they made me feel nervy and paranoid, so just the idea of taking pills—even medication prescribed by a doctor—skeeved me out. Plus, the possible side effects listed on many antidepressant drugs included "an increase in suicidal thoughts, insomnia, and general fatigue." *So let me get this straight,* I thought, *I'm going to take something that could make me feel more suicidal and out of my head?* Not a good plan. I couldn't afford to lose any more control over my mind. I was already in an emotionally 'effed-up state, so I challenged myself to take a more natural approach.

## The Straight Dope on Anxiety

I'm not a medical professional, so if you want the textbook definition of a generalized anxiety disorder, look it up. How I describe it is much simpler: anxiety happens when your mind spins out of control. It's an overall feeling of shittiness that triggers fear and excessive dread in your mind. I think it's actually a mental defense mechanism in which our mind "tells us" when we're being threatened. Problem is—anxiety triggers fear even when there is no *real* threat in sight. Anxiety manifests in many different ways. I suffer from both mental (an endless loop of negative smack talk in my head) and physical pain (headaches, fatigue, dizziness, sweating, and insomnia). When the anxiety becomes chronic, like 24/7, it feels like you're depressed—dark and low-down, all alone and powerless.

Both chronic anxiety and depression are serious conditions that, if left undiagnosed or untreated, can lead to super scary consequences. Be smart. Seek outside help if you think you need it. Seriously, I mean it. Anxiety isn't something to play around with or ignore. Trust me on this one.

---

I traded in my talk therapist for an *au naturel* social worker who gave me more-general advice I could relate to and immediately put into play. "You need to get reinvolved in your life," she told me. She suggested that the more involved I got in activities that forced me out of my bedroom bunker, the less time I'd have to focus on my anxious thoughts. This made sense to me, and as a temporary fix, it worked. I got a part-time job at the local newspaper, the *Staten Island Advance*. I slowly started working out at the gym again. And when the beginning of the next school semester came around, I enrolled at the local City University of New York branch, the CUNY College of Staten Island. A part of me really wanted to return to SUNY New Paltz, but I just didn't feel strong enough to leave home again. Not yet, anyway. Even though I'd gotten myself out of crisis mode, I was still a little freaked out. But I wasn't about to drop out of college altogether—getting a degree had always been an aspiration of mine and something I still really wanted to nail, so I decided that attending a school close to home would be the smartest move.

At the CUNY College of Staten Island, I majored in political science (I've always been a political nut). I also signed up for philosophy classes in an area called existentialism, which seeks to answer the very same questions that I'd been asking myself for months: *Why are we here? What's the point?* And you know what? It helped to discuss these "meaning of life" questions in public, outside of my own head, in a classroom filled with other kids wondering about the same things. I discovered, too, that many of history's best-known philosophers, like Plato and Aristotle, along with well-known thought leaders, like Abraham Lincoln and Albert Einstein, also suffered from a general sense of dread and sometimes even despair. What can I say—great minds think alike!

The more I learned, the better I started to feel. I was inspired by the existentialist focus on individual freedom, personal choice, and responsibility. The idea that the individual is a "self-determining agent" responsible for his or her choices really spoke to me. I began to wonder, *Do I have the power to stop this flood of anxious thoughts in my head? Can I choose to feel better?* The idea that I may have untapped power and control over my mind began to take root.

By the time I graduated from CUNY with a bachelor's degree in political science and a minor in Italian (and with magna cum laude and Phi Beta Kappa honors, thank you very much), I felt like

I'd gotten a handle on my anxiety. I'd continued to take my social worker's advice; by focusing my energy on work, school, my family, and getting in physical shape, I'd slowly chipped away at the negativity that nearly four years earlier had threatened to permanently take over my mind. Getting busy had proved to be the medicine I needed. I was confident again, and I was sure I was back in control.

Right after graduation, I took the LSAT and started an internship with a local Staten Island state assemblyman. I helped out around the office, wrote letters to Democratic constituents, and tagged along to cool political events. I had big plans to get a law degree, but then around the same time, a close friend of mine heard that MTV was casting a new reality TV show with ties to the Jersey Shore. An Italian American who grew up on Staten Island, I'd spent most of my summers on the Shore, so naturally I was tempted to apply.

I get it, this sounds like an 180-degree turn off my professional path, but a role on national television appealed to my creative, performer side. I've always been a bookish kid who made decent grades, but I also love to draw, write, rap, and act. For as long as I can remember, I've gotten the biggest kick out of cracking up my friends and family. Making them laugh gives me a natural high. So in addition to dreaming about getting a fancy law degree, I also fantasized about working in the entertainment industry.

Close friends and family knew this about me, so every once in a while, they'd send me links to random auditions in my area, and this time a link took me to a casting call for a reality show looking for "tan, muscled guidos who party at the Shore." This made me laugh. While I was no stranger to partying at the Shore, my pale, skinny-soft physique did not fit the description of the guy they were looking for. On the application form, I said things about myself like: "I have no tan, no spiky hair, and no muscles. I graduated college with a 3.9

GPA and come from a great Italian family . . . but I still love to party at the Shore!" For whatever reason, I landed an interview. My only guess is that the producers were intrigued to meet a different "breed" of guido.

The interview was conducted in a small hotel room in Seaside that smelled like hot sweat and regret. I'd had a couple of swigs of vodka before I walked in the door and gave the funniest interview of my life. I really let my wild side come out. I talked about girls, partying, fighting, and fist pumping (a prerequisite for partying at the Shore, I told them). I had them rolling on the floor laughing. The next thing I knew, I was on a plane to Los Angeles to meet the executive producer of the show. Here I was, this fresh-faced kid right out of college who rarely left New York, traveling to Los Angeles to impress some studio exec. At that point, I really didn't know anything about the show. There wasn't even a title for it yet. It was just a Hollywood "idea" and a long-shot opportunity for me, but I decided, *What the hell. Why not go for it?*

My trip was a calamity of errors. My plane got delayed in Phoenix, I had to hitchhike from the airport to the interview, and I showed up without a minute to spare. I was later told that if I'd arrived just five minutes later, the executive producer would have cut me from the list of possible candidates. But I made it just in time. I went in and killed it, and you know the rest—I became one of eight cast members on *Jersey Shore*. What I didn't know then was that the gig I'd just landed—where cameras follow you around all day, where friends and family aren't allowed to visit, where I wouldn't have access to a cell phone, TV, or radio for weeks—was a worst-case scenario for someone whose stress levels can easily spiral out of control.

# THE FIGHT AIN'T OVER

I was really pissed and disappointed in myself when I started feeling my anxiety resurface during the filming of the first season of *Jersey Shore*. After waking up to my first anxiety attack on set, I remember thinking, *Really? What the f\*ck! I thought I kicked this thing, and now this shit is back when I've been given one of the coolest opportunities of my life—you're gonna come f\*ck with me now?* The idea that the same anxiety that had paralyzed me in college was back terrified me. Not only that, I also worried that if the physical signs of my anxiety, like sweating and fidgety nervousness, came through on camera—*people are gonna see this shit, and then I'm screwed.*

I'd done a great job of dealing with my anxiety for the past four-plus years back home by refocusing my attention on getting good grades, working part-time, and hanging out with supportive friends and family. But suddenly I realized that I hadn't fixed the problem. I'd just temporarily buried it. Once again away from home, out of my element and thrown into a stressful environment, my anxiety had me back in a vicious headlock.

Well, I couldn't run away this time. I was on a locked friggin' set with cameras rolling on me all day long. I had to find a way to cope. I reached out to the resident therapist on set, who gave me a crash course on calming nerves (it turned out that I wasn't the first guy on a reality TV show who needed to relax). "Dr. B," who just exudes a cool, calm vibe, provided me with a few mental tricks to help me get through the 24/7 shooting schedule. I still felt like crap, but his simple mind tricks helped to pull me out of my hole and get through the first season without looking like a maniac who'd lost it. Even I'm fooled when I look back at those early episodes. Though I come off kinda shy, I basically look like a kid who's having a good time. You really have to dig deep into my eyes to see the truth. I'm freaking out on the inside. I'm terrified and trying like hell not to show it.

After season 1 of the show wrapped, I returned home with a very clear purpose—to get a handle on my anxiety, for good. Enough was enough! It was time to put a reliable program into place. I'd already been approached to shoot a second season of *Jersey Shore* in Miami, and without an action plan that I could take on the road, I knew I'd have to opt out and quit the show.

So what did I do?

First, I surrounded myself with a "dream team." I can't say enough about how important it is to surround yourself with supportive people whom you love and trust and who have your back, especially when you're feeling low. At the time, my team consisted of my older sister, Antonella, and my cousin Doug. My sister is the crunchy-granola type. She's vegan, practices yoga, and is a huge fan of eating and living right. Plus she battles with her own version of anxiety. She gets me, and she gets *it*. My cousin Doug is no stranger to dark days, either. The first time I tagged along with him to a standing-room-only AA meeting on Staten Island, I was hit with the realization that we've all got *something* we're struggling with. Doug, who's been addicted to alcohol and every drug on the street, has endured setbacks that would have buried the average guy, yet he still continues to show up to life, one hundred percent. He gave me the courage to fight, and to trust that if I needed him, he'd always have my back. He'd say to me, "Vinny, it's like you've got a fly buzzing around in your head that won't leave. I get it. But trust me, kid—you're going to be all right." Both Doug and Antonella supported me unconditionally, without any pressure or judgment. In many ways, they saved my life.

With my dream team in place, I started reading every inspirational pamphlet Doug brought home from his AA meetings. From there, I turned to popular books on personal growth, motivation, and spirituality by some of the most popular masters in the field. I devoured these books, sometimes three at a time. The more I read, the better I felt; I began to feel a connection to an inner power, an inner cool. As the stack of books in my bedroom grew (see my reading list at the back of this book) a very clear message began to emerge that became the baseline of my program: It was my own mind—not my circumstances—that was tripping me up the most. In other words, it wasn't the school environment. It wasn't the reality TV set or anyone or anything outside of me that was making me crazy. Rather, I'd gotten into a nasty habit of negative *thinking* that was triggering my anxiety. Until I learned how to flip the switch by retraining and regaining control of my own mind, my anxiety would continue to rule my life.

I credit guys like Wayne W. Dyer, Eckhart Tolle, and Deepak Chopra, among others, for teaching me some sick mental and physical tricks for calming my anxious mind. I modified many of their key teachings and techniques and developed a few of my own, and after several months of putting them into practice in a variety of situations, I created my no-bullshit program for controlling the crazy and getting my life back on track.

What you'll find in the pages ahead is *that* program. And while I created this mind-body-spirit triple-threat program to specifically battle my own anxiety and the occasional dip into depression, it's designed to tackle challenges that most everyone can relate to: stress, tension, worry, nervousness, frustration, sadness, and everyday negativity and low-down moods.

Am I cured? No. I freely admit it—I'm not immune to the occasional knockdown. Case in point: season 5 of *Jersey Shore* hit me like a right hook out of nowhere. That said, I wasn't down for long, and that's because I've found a way to get through it. While I still struggle from time to time, I have the strength and the strategies in place to pick myself back up off the floor and jump back into the ring. I won't be defeated.

And *listen up*—neither will you.

# PART TWO

# MY TRIPLE-THREAT PROGRAM

# MIND

# 1
# COOL YOUR EGO

**W**hen I went looking for a way to tackle my anxiety, I discovered that if I could simply master my mind—that is, get a handle on all my mad, crazy thoughts—I could actually control my crappy feelings, rather than letting them control me. I call this trick "controlling the crazy." Once *you* learn how to silence the crazy, negative noise in your own head, you can free yourself from feeling bad and focus on feeling good instead. It's amazing. Controlling the mind is not easy, but trust me, with a little work it's possible.

In this chapter, "Cool Your Ego," I'll tell you what I know about:

- Getting a handle on your thoughts

- The role the ego plays in your life

- How to spot an egomaniac

- How to shut down thoughts and feelings that make you crazy

## A Runaway Train

As I searched for information on how to get a handle on my anxious, stressed-out mind, I stumbled upon a study that says the average person has between twenty-five thousand and fifty thousand thoughts a day. That's a mad amount of thoughts, right? If most of these thoughts fall into the negative category—worrisome, fearful, sad, stressed, or generally low-down—you don't have to be a friggin' genius to realize that's *a lot* of negative thinking.

Imagine our heads consumed with that much garbage on any given day. That's how I felt during my first semester away at college. Everywhere I turned, a crazy thought seemed to be staring me in the face. I couldn't escape the garbage in my head, and this kicked off my anxiety—big-time. I later learned that when negative thoughts pile up like trash in your mind, they cause negative *feelings* like fear, insecurity, stress, anger, anxiety, and even depression. Most people think it happens the other way around. They say, "I'm anxious" or "I'm stressed" or "I'm feeling down, and that's why my head's full of dark and draining thoughts." Nope. That's not how it works. You feel weighed down and low *because* of your thoughts. And it doesn't stop there.

Like a runaway train, negative thoughts create negative *feelings,* and those feelings trigger negative *behaviors*. In the reality TV world, I see this happen all the time. Someone believes they've been wronged, this turns into anger, and the next thing you know, a fist goes through the wall, a bottle or a spatula gets thrown across the room. See how that works? First you lose control over your mind. Next you inevitably lose control over your feelings and actions.

## You're the Conductor

What you choose to think about has a direct effect on your feelings and emotions, your behaviors and actions. Yeah, I said *choose*. Because thinking seems to happen automatically, we're often unaware that we choose our thoughts. But it's the truth. Each thought that enters your mind you've actually *invited* to be there, which means that you're in control of what goes on in your head one hundred percent of the time. In other words, you can choose to feel anxious and stressed or upbeat and optimistic. You're the friggin' conductor of the train! You're in control, and you, and you alone, can stop the negative momentum of your mind. How? Keep reading.

Because the thoughts that get you down are just creations of your mind, you have sick odds of beating back crappy, negative feelings by simply changing how you think. For real, changing your thoughts is the fastest way to change how badly you feel. This is good news because feelings, we all know, aren't easy to control. I've found out the hard way that once you get into the ring with fear, insecurity, anger, worthlessness, and judgment, you might as well throw in the towel. Bad feelings will beat you down every time, which is why it's important to cut them off at the thought level. And that's exactly what I'm going to teach you how to do.

In my program, the first actionable step toward changing how you think is becoming fully aware of how your mind "talks" to you.

# Tune In

Over the next twenty-four hours, keep a running tally of the thoughts that nag you. Tune in and take notice of the thoughts that *really* consume you, the ones that really speak the loudest, go round and round in your head, and hang around.

Keep track of these thoughts in a journal or on your smartphone or personal computer. Ask yourself, *How much of my thinking is focused on the negative side of life?* For example, do you focus on what's wrong, what could go wrong, what already *went* wrong—and ignore what's going right? Do you jump to conclusions and often assume the worst? Do you fall into the trap of all-or-nothing, black-and-white thinking, where you tell yourself things like *I'll never have a boyfriend/girlfriend* or *I'll always be broke and in debt*? How often do you think critical thoughts about other people? Track your thoughts over a twenty-four-hour period, and as you do, try to resist the urge to judge or have an opinion about any of them. Simply write them down.

A little bit further into the program, you'll learn how to flip your thoughts upside down from negative to positive, but for now, just recognize how often you think the worst.

If this exercise feels like a downer to you, lighten your mood by laughing at the thoughts that make you feel low. I'm serious. Laugh out loud at them. Sometimes our thoughts are so stupid, they're actually hilarious. I often say to myself, *Vin, where do you come up with this shit?* When I can laugh at how ridiculous my thoughts are, they don't bring me down as much. They lose their power over me.

Many of the big-time spiritual masters refer to this discipline as "observing" the thinker, where one watches one's thoughts like clouds passing by. Eckhart Tolle says in *The Power of Now,* "You'll soon realize: there is the voice, and here I am listening to it, watching it." What I like about this image is the idea behind it—that our thoughts are actually something to be observed. Meaning, they're separate from us.

## Mind Games

Most of us have self-identified with what our minds have to say for so long, we believe without question that the rambling dialogue inside our heads is the voice of our true self talking. Nope. The voice in your head that makes you feel afraid, anxious, insecure, stressed out, and angry is not your *true* voice; it's not *You*. It's just your mind running wild, and you can choose whether or not you want to listen to the wild rant and also what to believe.

---

### HOLD UP

### The True You

From here on out, I will refer to your true voice and who you truly are as *You*. For example, the voice inside your head that triggers your biggest fears, insecurities, and mad anger isn't really *You*—it's just your mind running wild.

Not sure you get it? Just go with it. Thinking about your mind and your thoughts as separate from who *You* really are may sound crazy (it did to me at first), and while your gut reaction might be to call bullshit, at least try to entertain the idea. Don't discount what I'm saying just because you've never thought this way before. The ideas I discuss in this chapter may take some getting used to, so try not to overthink them. Just be open, and be patient if you don't immediately "get" what I'm saying. Funny enough, the less you think about thinking, the more it'll start to make sense.

---

Okay, we're gonna drill down into this idea a little more. Start by answering this question: where do you think your thoughts come from? That's right—your mind. But what you might not know is that your mind has a *mind* of its own. It's an independent agent with its own agenda; you'd be smart to be suspicious of it. While your mind can be a very useful and amazing tool, if it's allowed to run wild and unchecked, like mine has a tendency to do, it can really mess you up.

The majority of your nervous, anxious, frustrated, and fearful thoughts are created by a part of your mind called the ego. To understand how the ego works, imagine that your mind is a computer—your desktop, laptop, BlackBerry, or iPad. Your computer helps you do important things like multitask, create order, make decisions, and solve problems. It's efficient and helpful. You can't imagine life without it. In fact, your computer is your best friend—until it gets infected by a virus. Then, it's as if you can't function at all. You're lost! The same can be said about your ego. It's like a virus in your mind. When your mind is infected by your ego—the critical, negative voice in your head—you can quickly lose your ability to function and behave in a way that positively benefits you and the people around you.

Discussions on the ego can sometimes get super confusing. The first time I heard the word *ego,* I thought of the song "Ego," by Kanye West and featuring Beyoncé Knowles. Kanye sings about having a "big ego" and equates it with being overly confident and well endowed. While I dig the song, Kanye misses the mark. No disrespect, Kanye, but having an ego involves more than a cocky attitude.

## The Ego

Think of your ego as the critical voice inside your head that's been there as long as you can remember it. It's the voice behind your most nagging, negative, and anxious thoughts. It's the one that complains, gossips, and judges. It's also the voice that triggers your biggest fears and insecurities and makes you defensive, angry, and resentful. It blames others, fuels conflicts, argues, and causes drama. No, I'm not talking about your mother-in-law. You're probably too polite to say it, so I will—this voice can be a real whiny prick. Not only that, but for many of us, it seems to constantly be in our ear, available 24/7 to provide running commentary and mental movies about the doom of the future and the past. This voice can be crazy making!

Just in case you're wondering—having a "voice" in your head doesn't mean you have a split personality and need a shrink. It actually means you're normal. We *all* have a voice like this. Because you spend so much time listening to this voice, you identify with it, like it's a part of you or is *You*. But your ego is simply a truckload of thoughts and feelings you've been carting around your whole life. And those thoughts and feelings aren't really *You*—they're just garbage your mind has created. Am I making sense?

Certainly not everything you think about falls into the garbage pile, but when it comes to the thoughts your ego creates, I can't think of a better way of describing them. Not only does your ego encourage negative thinking, it thrives on it. Some spiritual teachers go so far as to compare the ego with a parasite that uses your mind as a host, feeding on your crappy thoughts and biggest fears. The crappier your thoughts, the stronger your ego becomes. And if you're like me and have a tendency to be anxious, stressed, and generally full of gloom and doom, your ego's grown so fat and powerful it looms over you like some bloodthirsty predator in a sci-fi horror film. Yeah, I know, this might be a little over the top, but now you get the picture, right?

## Egomaniac

To beat back your ego, you have to start by recognizing that your ego is actually separate from the true *You*. It turns out that *You* are so much more than what goes through your head; it's just that you've been listening to and taking direction from your ego for so long that you've lost touch with your true voice. In the next chapter, "Get Real," I'll discuss what your true voice sounds like, but before we go there, I want you to get clear on the kind of noise your ego makes. The following mental workout will help you do just that.

### VINNY'S MENTAL WORKOUT

### Give Your Ego a Name

Did you ever see the 1991 cult classic *Drop Dead Fred,* starring Phoebe Cates as Lizzie and Rik Mayall as her imaginary childhood friend Fred? In the movie, Lizzie is harassed by Fred, who constantly talks to her and incites her to do things that create drama and chaos in her life.

A parallel can be drawn between Fred and your ego. Over your lifetime, your ego, the loudmouth that rules your head, has become so dominant and strong, it's like it's taken on a life of its own and become its own person—a character like the one in *Drop Dead Fred*. You've come to identify this character as your "self." But that's not really *You*. It's more like your stand-in self, or some douchey spokesperson you hired to represent you. Believe it or not, you have another "self," which sounds and acts very different from your ego. To differentiate between the two, you need to create a mental image of your ego and give it a name. (I call mine "The Douche Bag" or "The Hater.")

Create a picture of your ego in your mind. What does he or she look like? What kind of things has he or she said to you today? How have those thoughts influenced your mood? Your interactions with other people? Your behavior in general? Begin to notice when your ego talks to you and how it influences you. Call it out by name.

The purpose of naming and creating a mental image of your ego is to make it easily recognizable to you. Once you're able to recognize your ego as separate from *You,* you can begin to detach from it. This is the main objective of my program: to eventually free you from your ego, the voice that provides negative running commentary that hijacks your mood, your behavior, your relationships, and your *life*!

I don't know about you, but the idea that the garbage in your head is just a creation of your mind—and not really *You*—is one of the most empowering ideas I've ever come across. It saved me! I spent so many anxious nights in college pacing back and forth in my dorm room and taking frantic walks around campus sweating, crying, and feeling lost and alone. Looking back, I realize that I was trying to run away from my own mind. My ego had a vicious hold on me; I felt like I was being held hostage by my own thoughts. I felt crazy, out of control, and terrified, which only made the presence of my ego even stronger. Once I realized that I could detach from my ego, "The Douche Bag," I felt like a prisoner who'd been set free.

If you're like me, once you become aware of your own ego, you will easily begin to recognize the ego in other people. To get started, check out how people around you carry themselves. Do they have attitude? Are they touchy, jumpy, cocky, bitchy, whiny, gossipy, bossy, or petty? If so, you've just spotted an egomaniac, someone who's letting his or her own ego influence his or her actions, reactions, and interactions with other people.

If you're ever in doubt that you're dealing with someone ruled by his or her ego, here's a short list of obvious giveaways. You'll notice that he or she:

- Brings mad drama to every situation

- Is constantly in need of attention

- Finds fault in other people; gossips

- Holds a grudge

- Judges and criticizes his or her own actions; has low self-esteem

- Is easily offended

- Reacts defensively

- Is fearful, worried, and anxious

- Likes to always be right and acts superior

- Pushes his or her agenda—the bossy type

- Behaves in a controlling way—the bully type

# IN THE REAL WORLD: Bullies, the Worst Kind of Egomaniac

The bully is a perfect example of someone ruled by his or her ego.

When I was sixteen, I was a busboy in an Italian restaurant. For those of you who don't know how the restaurant hierarchy works, the busboy is the lowest on the food chain, next to the dishwasher. Knowing this well, the more senior waiters would constantly boss me around and bully me for being young, naive, and—in their eyes—insignificant! I remember the first day on the job, the older headwaiter asked me if I knew what a "monkey dish" was, and when I said no, he rolled his eyes and shook his head at me like I was an idiot.

They liked to throw in my face how much older and more experienced they were, and how much money they were making. Now, looking back, I can see clearly that these guys were operating from their egos. Their own insecurities, fears, resentments, and judgments were in front of their actions. I can only guess, but maybe they'd been picked on at some point when they were just starting out, and years later, they were taking it out on me. Who knows, but what I now know for sure is that their negative shit had everything to do with what was going on in their own heads and nothing to do with me. That's the case with most bullies.

- Is never satisfied; always wants more

- Is overly concerned with what others think of him or her

- Is typically a buzzkill and not much fun to be around

These behaviors tell you straightaway that you're dealing with a person who's allowing his or her ego to run his or her life. Interacting with an egomaniac can be tough work. The ego loves company. It's a master at drawing people into its sick web. If some egomaniac is projecting toxic energy my way, I must be strong and fight off the impulse to get drawn into his negativity. If I feel myself getting worked up and defensive, I know this is *my* ego talking—egging me into conflict. At that point, I have a decision to make: I can either submit to the thoughts swirling around in my head, tell this guy he's an idiot, and allow the situation to escalate, *or* I can recognize that the negative narration in my head is *not really me*. Furthermore—and this is key—I must acknowledge that what's coming out of d-bag's mouth is *not really him*. It's just *his* ego talking. You see, when you can separate a person's ego from who he or she truly is, you can never be hurt by what a person says or does.

## IN THE REAL WORLD: It's Not About You

If someone says something ugly to you, recognize that's just his or her ego making noise. His or her judgment has nothing to do with you. Sure, it may be directed *at* you, but it's not about you. Understand the difference? Don't take other people's garbage personally. When you don't take offense or react to someone's negativity, you disarm your opponent and de-escalate the conflict. You win by doing nothing!

Notice that while egomaniacs are not fun to be around (and in some cases, they can be straight-up assholes), if you're able to take a step back and recognize their behaviors as the unavoidable by-product of all the negative shit that's piled up in their own heads, it's easier to feel compassion for them. Bottom line: they're suffering and need help. At some point, if they don't separate from that ego of theirs, they'll likely find themselves in a very dark and lonely place. But helping others avoid their own pitfall is not your work right now. Controlling your own crazy is, so let's get back to it.

Before we go any further, take a moment here and own up. Is your ego running the show? Do you recognize yourself in the short list of egomaniac behaviors? On a good day, maybe not, but on a bad day—yes? If your ego is getting in your way (which it does for most people), then read on. You're in the right place.

You've taken a powerful first step by becoming aware of your thoughts. Now let's kick it up a notch and cool your ego, bro. What do I mean by that? In addition to becoming mindful of what goes on in your head, you'll want to start to notice how often you take direction from your ego. In other words, how much of your *behavior* is triggered by the crazy-making thoughts running wild in your head? The easiest way to determine this is by paying attention to your conversations, interactions with, and reactions to other people.

## VINNY'S MENTAL WORKOUT

## Cool Your Ego

Over the next few days, become mindful of your conversations, interactions with, and reactions to other people. For example, do you catch yourself trying to control situations and sometimes other people? Do you become defensive with friends, family, and colleagues? How about with the barista at the coffee shop, the girl who checks you in at the gym, or the guy in the car lane next to you? Are you easily annoyed? Offended? Provoked into an argument or a fight? When you're talking with people, do you catch yourself defending, blaming, criticizing, or judging? How important is it for you to be right? How attached are you to your opinions? In other words, how attached are you to your *ego*? Is your ego running the show?

Remember that your thoughts make a direct play on your emotions, so if you're feeling angry, for example, try tracing your anger back to its original thought. Pretend like you're some crime scene investigator from *CSI: Las Vegas.* Trace your anger back to the thought or thoughts that set you off.

Try this mental workout several times over the next few days and see what you come up with. Pay close attention to your mood, to your interactions with other people, and to the thoughts that came before them.

---

You may also notice that the thoughts that trigger a negative emotional reaction like stress, worry, or frustration also *physically* weaken you. Get this: strong thoughts and feelings often show up in our physical bodies. If you've ever had a stress headache or an anxious stomach, then you know exactly what I'm talking about. My anxiety likes to show up as tension headaches that make my head feel like it's being squeezed by a vise.

When we wrapped filming season 4 of *Jersey Shore* in Florence, Italy, we went straight to New Jersey to film season 5. This meant another six weeks of shooting without getting a break. It was exhausting and set off my anxiety in a major way. When I traced the stress headache and sick feeling in my stomach back to my thoughts, what I found going round and round in my head was: *I won't get to see my family. I'll be cut off from everyone for another six weeks. I won't get a break. I'm gonna lose it.*

As you become more mindful of the thoughts going on in your head on a regular basis, also become aware of the noise that not only mentally brings you down but also threatens to physically weaken you. In a later chapter, I'll teach you how to tackle that kind of noise head-on.

## Shut It Down

In addition to feeling super charged and empowered by the idea that my thoughts are separate from me was the even sicker discovery that I could learn to shut them down, much like you'd shut down a laptop. Before I learned how to shut them down, I'd try to "think" my way out of my anxious 'effed-up mood. This never worked. Why? Because thinking and *overthinking* is the problem! To cool your ego and put negativity in check, you must use a combination of tricks and techniques that give your brain the slip. The following is the first of many exercises I use to do just that.

**VINNY'S MENTAL WORKOUT**

### Give Your Mind the Slip

The quickest way I've learned to shut down my overly anxious mind is to focus on what's happening *right here, right now*. Every so often when my mind's running wild, I'll take a break from whatever I'm doing—working out at the gym, packing for a club appearance, getting ready to head out for a night—and I'll take a seat and close my eyes. I take several deep breaths in and out, and then, when I open my eyes, I focus on the moment—what's going on *right here, right now*. Is it morning, afternoon, or evening? What does the light look like outside? What do I hear? Are people talking? Is the room quiet? What do I smell? My mom's home cooking on the stove? How do I feel? Is my body relaxed and loose, or tight from the gym?

For two to three minutes, I concentrate only on what I can immediately see, hear, smell, and touch. This may sound simple enough to do, but trust me—it takes a lot of concentration and practice. Our minds love to jump back and forth between the past and the future. We have a hard time *sitting still*.

Give it a try. Take a break from reading this page right now and concentrate on what's going on around you. If your mind drifts back to what you were doing an hour ago or skips forward to your plans for later today or tomorrow, refocus on the here and now. When you focus on the present moment, you'll find that your ego, the voice that triggers your darkest thoughts, stops making noise.

*Ahhhh*, the peace and quiet!

The first time I tried this was in my backyard on Staten Island. I was feeling pretty bad. I'd just finished filming season 1 of *Jersey Shore*, and I was still waking up every day feeling scared, anxious, and confused. On this particular afternoon, my mind was going a mile a minute. I'd been asked by the producers of *Jersey Shore* to film a second season in Miami, and I was really worried I'd get there and freak and not be able to handle it. I was pacing around my house and finally walked outside to get some air. I sat down in a chair facing the sun and closed my eyes. I took a deep breath in and focused on how the warmth of the sun and the breeze in the air felt on my skin. I tuned in to the sounds around me—birds chirping in the trees overhead, and my English bulldog, Jelly, huffing and puffing as he ran around the yard.

I know, the scene I'm describing sounds like some friggin' Snow White moment, and I'm almost embarrassed to recount it except for that it *worked*. It lasted for only a minute, if that, but while I was concentrating on the immediate world around me, my mind went blank. No more noise. No more worry. Just peace and calm, and the sense that everything was going to be okay. For those few split seconds, I realized I had the power to control the crazy. This felt like a huge accomplishment. I thought, *If it worked this one time, it can work again.* It was true: the practice can be repeated and improved.

## It Takes Practice

Noticing the right here, right now, may sound like a simple no-brainer exercise, but trust me—it takes practice. It may take several tries before you get it down, which is why you'll see it pop up in several of the next mental workouts. Once you've gotten the hang of it, I'll give you something more complex to master. My mental workouts build on one another, getting more advanced as you get further into the program, so be patient. Take it slow, and wait for the big payoff.

Just to be clear, I'm not saying you need to stop thinking altogether. I remember talking to a girl I was dating once about the power of shutting down one's thoughts, and she said, "Vinny, if I'm not thinking, then I'd be in, like, a *coma*." She couldn't understand how you could exist, function, or live without *thinking*. Let me assure you—this program is not about becoming a walking zombie.

It's about shutting down the negative thoughts that trigger mental, physical, and spiritual stress and get the best of you.

# What's Your Problem?

Once you're able to shut down your ego, you can do and accomplish amazing things. All the energy you've spent feeling bad is freed up for feeling *good*. (Not like the best sex of your life good. That's what I was expecting when I first learned about this practice. One of my favorite spiritual teachers, Eckhart Tolle, wrote that he sat on park benches for two years in euphoria enjoying the wonders of life. I can't promise you that, but I can promise that you'll feel better than you do now.)

Yet I'll warn you right now: your ego is going to put up a fight. Be prepared for mental warfare. The ego is in it to win it and is a master at defending itself. Don't be surprised if it starts talking mad crazy in your ear, trying to convince you that quieting your mind is a very bad and scary thing. When I first started shutting my mind down in different situations, I'd get all freaked out and scared. At first I didn't understand why I was so afraid until it dawned on me how much time I regularly spent dwelling on and obsessing over things that were making me unhappy. My "problems" had become so familiar to me that I'd unconsciously wrapped them up in my idea of who I was—*I'm Vinny, the kid with chronic anxiety who feels like a freak.* I discovered that behind the fear of shutting down my mind—in effect, letting my problems *go*—was the worry, *If I no longer have this problem, then who am I?* I was having separation anxiety about separating my ego from my true self. You follow?

Conscious of it or not, on some level, most of us have become attached to our ego. The smack-talking voice in our heads is familiar, and what's familiar makes us feel safe. Feeling safe feels good, so we're protective of this voice—even when the things it says make us miserable. I know it sounds ass-backward and crazy, but that's simply the way we work. Think about the girl who keeps breaking up with her jerk-off boyfriend, only to land back in bed with him a week later. She knows he's bad for her, but they've been together off and on for years. He's familiar; he's what she *knows*. The unknown is risky, so even though he lies to her and treats her like dog shit, she still regards him as a safe bet, and so she keeps him around.

Many of us have similarly created a sick and twisted attachment to the voice that tells us it's okay to hold on to shitty situations and toxic people that make us feel stressed, scared, and low-down. Just like it is with the girl who stays with the wrong guy, maintaining the attachment to your ego will hurt you. For real, this is the truth. And when your ego uses its manipulative ways to try to convince you that shutting down the crazy rant is the same as shutting down who you are, don't fall for it. This is bullshit. Remember: your negative thoughts are not *You,* and your problems don't define *You.*

# Moving On . . .

So, if I'm not my thoughts, then who or *what* am I? Good question. Underneath all the negative garbage that clogs your airwaves on a daily basis is your *true* self, the real *You.* In the next chapter, "Get Real," you'll learn how to tap in to and listen to the real *You.* Once you do that, you'll access an inner power that can stop the negative momentum of your mind dead in its tracks.

# 2
# GET REAL

Think about the last time you thought something negative about yourself. Now consider this: *You* are so much more than the negative, crazy-mad thoughts that run through your head.

For real, *You* are a lot more than the things that randomly go through your mind every day—both negative and positive. So just because your mind has "said" something about you doesn't make it true. Once you believe this, you open yourself up to discover who *You* truly are—a fire, a spark, a light, or as Katy Perry sings, a firework.

What I've come to understand is that on the inside, we're all positive energy and light. Your inner light isn't something you can dress up for a night out at the clubs; it's invisible, yet it's still very much alive inside you, and the evidence of its existence is that you *feel* it. Some people refer to this light as your soul or spirit, your "authentic," "real," or "best" self. I call it the true self—who *You* truly are.

In this chapter, "Get Real," you'll come to understand more about who *You* are, and once you do, you'll access a power that gives you positive control over your life. In addition, I'll tell you what I know about:

- The difference between *You* and your "social costume"

- How to tap in to your inner power

- The trick to getting in the zone

- Ways to improve your relationships

- How to spark your creativity

- The key to boosting your confidence

Believe it or not, *You* are much bigger and more powerful than your ego and its negative trash talk. Like I said before, it's just that you've gotten into such a regular habit of listening to your ego, you've forgotten who *You* truly are. Not to worry. My program is all about reconnecting to your true self.

*You* came into this world with a strong and powerful energy that's free of negativity, that's egoless. Think about it—most babies aren't born with anxiety and stress. They aren't easily offended, defensive, pushy, or controlling. Babies aren't interested in any of that bullshit. No, people call them "little bundles of joy" because that's what they are! They're pure, peaceful, positive energy. And that's what *You* are—still. Believe it or not, buried underneath the critical, combative voice of your ego, you speak another language—the language of feeling totally cool, calm, content, and positively in control.

Think of it this way: your *true self* is like a deep, waveless ocean, while your ego is the raging sea. When you imagine the bottom of the ocean, it's tranquil and steady, right? There could be a nuclear war going on above the surface, but the deep ocean floor remains relatively unchanged and still. Who *You* are on the inside is as calm and peaceful as the deep ocean floor. You may be feeling mad crazy on the surface, but the steady calm I'm describing exists inside you at all times. It's mad powerful, and it's *always* available to you. You just have to learn how to access it.

**HOLD UP**

## Don't Get Hung Up

I've started to use words and lingo like *ego, true self,* and *inner power* that you might qualify as self-help mumbo jumbo. My advice: Don't get hung up on the words. If they distract you or turn you off in any way, feel free to substitute words you like better. Don't make it an issue.

## Social Costume

Deep down, I'm sure you know that there's more to *You* than meets the eye. Yet it's very easy to ignore what's underneath when all you can see is the surface. For example, on the surface you may be some twenty-six-year-old guy who drives a Benz and has fifty pairs of shoes and an apartment with three flat-screen TVs. Sweet for you, but whatever. None of this stuff defines *You*. It's just stuff that helps people label you. It gives you a "social costume" to wear.

Most of us wear a social costume when we go out into the world, and it's these costumes that give us our identity. They also divide and separate us. I don't care if you're in high school, college, or the professional world, what kind of education you have, religion you practice, or what neighborhood you live in—you more than likely fall into some kind of group, posse, or social scene based on your social costume. When I was in high school, there were the emos, the jocks, the gangsters, and the Twilight kids. Now that I'm in my twenties, I'm surrounded by the guidos at the Shore, the hipsters in Brooklyn, and the juice bags at the gym. These are just roles people play, the costumes they wear. I play the role of the TV reality star, the guido, and the mama's boy. Now don't get me wrong. Wearing a social costume isn't necessarily a bad thing. In many ways, our social costume is how we relate to the people around us. Your social costume becomes a problem only when you forget that it's just that—a costume, something you're wearing on the outside that covers up what's underneath.

You may not even be aware that you wear a social costume to work or school every day, and can you guess why? Your ego—the whiny and insecure voice in your head—has got you convinced that you need a social costume to survive—that you're nothing without it! Your ego has you believing that your achievements and awards define you. That who *You* are is what you have, whom you know, how you dress, and what you weigh. Because your competitive ego is consumed with what other people think, it's constantly comparing you with everyone around you, rating your looks, your performance, and your *life* on a brutal scale of 1 to 10. Your ego is the voice behind social pressure. And I probably don't need to tell you—it's persuasive! But this voice isn't always right. Remember, this voice isn't even *You*. It's just your mind talking shit.

## Social Costume

Deepak Chopra in *The Seven Spiritual Laws of Success* says the ego "is not who you really are. The ego is your self-image; it is the role you are playing." Chopra's idea of one's self-image is what I call your "social costume." Your upbringing, lifestyle, education, social standing, and zip code all play into the costume you wear. Yet who you are on the outside is often very different from who *You* truly are on the inside. Take Britney Spears, for example. Do you think Britney is the girl you see on stage? No way. Her pop image is not who she *really* is. She's just a person like you and me. And whether she knows it or not, her true power comes from within, not from her trademark miniskirt and grinding dance moves.

---

Like I said, I wear a social costume too. It's kind of hard to avoid when you're in a business where image rules, where what you wear and how you act is constantly caught on camera and scrutinized on *TMZ* and Twitter. When I'm at a big Hollywood event like the Video Music Awards, there are gangster rappers, reality stars, actors, and singers all competing on the surface. They brag over who's invited to the dopest afterparties, who's wearing the most expensive watch, who's got the biggest boobs and the best designer dress. Again, don't get me wrong—having nice things and being the best dressed can be awesome. (Yours truly was one of the best dressed at the 2011 VMAs, according to *GQ*!) But it can't *define* you. When the big event is over, when the club appearance, Knicks game, or video game release party has come to an end and I'm back in my hotel room or at home on Staten Island, I know who I really am. Underneath the hat, the clothes, and the shades I'm just a twenty-four-year-old kid, no better, no worse than anyone else. I'm not my achievements, my celebrity status, or my money. I'm not my ego. I'm just pure positive light and energy. My real power comes from within, and it's as cool, calm, and steady as the deep ocean floor.

## BREAK IT DOWN

## Your Inner Power

*You* have an inner power. This "power" can't necessarily be explained, so try not to overanalyze it! It cannot be thought about or comprehended by the mind. The only proof of its existence is that you *feel* it. And when you do, when you experience *You*—you feel cool, calm, steady, and positively powerful and in control. For real, *You* have sick power, and once you tap in to it, you can accomplish just about anything. Your potential is limitless.

Think (but don't overthink) about the difference between the social costume that you wear and your true self this way: you could be driving a brand-new Ferrari or a broken-down Toyota—no matter—it doesn't change who *You* really are. Having a nice ride is fine, and if you're driving one—good for you. But just know that *You* aren't your car, your fake boobs, your Rolex, or your Gucci shoes. What you wear and how you act on the outside doesn't change the fact that your true power comes from within.

**VINNY'S MENTAL WORKOUT**

# Who You Are Is Who You're Not

Take out a piece of paper and list all the things that define you on a surface level. For example, maybe you're Joe Blow, a twenty-two-year-old guy with a college degree who just landed a job in the gaming industry—props to you! You hope to soon be making over $75,000 a year, and you have your eyes set on a new BMW. You've already hit on the hot chick in glasses who sits across from your cube at work, and you're convinced you'll have her number by the end of the week. Life is looking pretty good for you right now.

On the flip side, maybe you're Stacy Smacey, a sixteen-year-old high school student with weight issues who isn't loving life so much. You sit at the table with the theater geeks in school. You're totally smart but spend all your time obsessing about what it would be like to be skinny, popular, and accepted by the cool kids.

Write down everything that defines your "image," or "social costume," and once you feel that your list is complete, I want you to crumple it up and throw it across the room.

Now who are you left with? Did you just say *nobody*? Not true. When you strip off your social costume, you're left with *You*! *You*, in your purest form! Get it? The question to ask is not who you are, but who you're not. You're not what you've achieved, who you know, what you wear, or how much you weigh. *You* are not any of that. *You* are a spark—a light—a positive and powerful force that cannot be measured or seen, but only *felt*.

My cousin Doug is one of the few people I know who doesn't confuse his social costume with who he truly is. In fact, if it's possible to be imageless, that's Doug. He's a thirty-five-year-old financially burdened, ex-alcoholic/junkie who can't afford shoes. He lives paycheck to paycheck in a crappy-ass apartment. I know this sounds sad, but he knows material things don't define his happiness, so I'm allowed to call him out. Trust me, he makes fun of himself! He really doesn't care *at all* what people think of him. Sometimes I take him to the most high-class clubs in New York City, and he whispers in my ear, "I'm the poorest person in here," and we both laugh hysterically. He's completely himself, and he makes no apologies about it. As far as I'm concerned, this makes him a hero, but he just shrugs me off. He says, "Vin, why do I want to get mixed up in all that stuff? Who cares? Just be yourself." It's easy for him. He's completely disconnected from his ego, the voice that likes to make comparisons and surface judgments. Doug just doesn't go there. His outsides match his insides, and he lives by the words of André Gide: "It's better to be hated for what you are than loved for what you are not."

Let's pause for a moment. I'm going to assume that, to some degree, the thought of stripping yourself of your social costume—the image you've created for yourself—has made you a little bit uncomfortable. Am I right? Do you feel naked? A little exposed and insecure? It's normal if you do. Most of us are afraid to let the world see us for who we truly are. We prefer to be defined by the costume we wear. Taking it off seems scary because having an "identity" makes us feel like we belong somewhere. (It's better to belong somewhere than *nowhere,* right?) I get that, but I want to let you in on a little secret—you're more powerful without it. Most people believe that their social costume gives them power, but it's a false power. True power comes from within.

# True Benefits

So, let's get real. What is this "power" I'm talking about, and how can you tap in to it? Gaining access to your inner power is easier than you might think; I've been to parties that are harder to get into, but before I show you how to tap in, let me first discuss the benefits of getting connected.

Earlier, I said that who *You* are on the inside is like the bottom of the deep ocean—calm, cool, and steady. Maybe you're thinking, *That sounds sweet, but how does being like the ocean floor help me in the real world?* I'll tell you. Once I learned how to turn down the mad noise in my head and tap in to my cool, calm inner power, I began to regain positive control over my life. My anxiety and stress had less of a hold on me, and for the first time in as long as I could remember, I felt indestructible, like I could accomplish anything— kinda like Bradley Cooper in the movie *Limitless,* where when he discovers NZT, a top-secret drug, he's suddenly able to accomplish *anything in record time.* Likewise, once you're able to shut down your ego and connect to the true *You,* you feel not only calm, cool, and chill, but also more aware and focused. Suddenly, you have the power to kill it in nearly every situation you can think of.

For example, imagine the craziest day in your life. Friends and colleagues are fighting, there is construction noise outside your window, or some loudmouth is talking right outside your door when you're trying to get work done. When you're connected to the cool, calm, steady power inside *You,* you're suddenly immune to all this annoying noise. It can't touch *You.* And if you haven't experienced that kind of power lately, let me assure you—it's solid gold. Think about all the ways that your noisy mind slows you down throughout your day, every day. Most of us spend a lot of time stuck in our heads, listening to our ego and letting the negative talk get in the way. This is a total time-suck—not to mention a complete waste of energy. Once you shut down the crazy thoughts, you can use that energy to access your inner power and get shit done. Seriously. I think you'll be surprised at what you're capable of.

## The Game-Changer

Once you shut down your ego, you'll discover that you're able to focus more easily. As a result, in everything you do—be it on a sports field, in the classroom, on the job, at school, on a stage, spitting game to a hot girl—you'll be able to make faster and more focused decisions. In other words: you're in a position to kick serious ass.

Think about basketball superstar Kobe Bryant for a minute. When the seconds are counting down and he knows he needs a turn-around jump shot to win the game, do you think his noisy mind is running that ball? No! The play that wins the game comes from a power inside him. When Kobe's "in the zone," he's out of his head and tapped in to his cool, calm, and steady inner power.

Now that I've started acting, I have to memorize lines for my roles. Most of the shows I've appeared in are filmed in Los Angeles, which for me is a very distracting place to work. The celebrity parties and events, the beautiful weather, and California girls make it very easy for me to lose focus. So when I'm out there for acting purposes, I know I have to get in *my* zone or else I'm going to blow it on set. Like you began to do in chapter 1, "Cool Your Ego," I give my mind the slip by focusing on the present, the *right here, right now*. When I'm present, I can fully concentrate on studying and memorizing my lines and preparing for my role. If negative thoughts or feelings like worry, anxiety, and stress begin to creep back into my head, throwing me off focus, I question the voice behind the thought. I call it out! For example, if I'm mentally preparing for an acting gig and an ego-based thought creeps into my head like *Vin—you're going to bomb it on set tomorrow,* I'll question it. I'll say, *Really? Who says? Why should I believe you? Where's your proof?* By calling my ego out, I stop senseless anxiety, stress, and doubt in its tracks and regain my focus. *I am* NOT *going to bomb on set tomorrow. I'm gonna kill it!* Remember, thoughts like *I can't* and *I suck* are just senseless talk your ego has dreamt up. Don't believe them. They're not real.

## Just Breathe

Later in the book, there's a whole chapter dedicated to breathing techniques, but I want to mention this practice early on so that you have something to do now, should your anxious mind be getting in the way of your ability to focus and get the job done. The simple act of breathing is one of the fastest and easiest ways I know of to quiet the mind and get present. I use it all the time. I call it my "emergency" tool.

When you arm yourself with tools to control your crazy *before* it has the chance to control you, then when you need them, you can simply pull them out of your back pocket and put them to work.

So, how does something as basic as breathing work to silence the ego? Easy. Close your eyes and breathe in deeply from your stomach until your lungs are good and full, and then slowly let your breath out. Do it again. The more you focus on your breath, the less you'll be able to focus on whatever's distracting, worrying, or bothering you. Breathing slows down the negative momentum of your runaway mind and parks you in the present moment. (Try breathing like this through every page of this book. Your mind will stop trying to overthink and overanalyze what you're reading, and before you know it, the ideas will just "click" into place.) What I also like about breathing is that not only does it work quickly, but you can do it anywhere, completely unnoticed. It's super smooth.

## The Bedroom Rock Star

This is a bit personal, but I've found that the practice of shutting down my anxious thoughts and connecting with my inner power has helped me out with women, especially in the bedroom. A lot of guys, myself included, get nervous when it comes to "performing." If a play-stopping negative thought goes through my head like *Oh boy, you have to get it up! She's gonna tell everyone you suck in bed . . . do it . . . do it . . . come on!!!,* I take a deep breath and acknowledge that these are just ego-driven thoughts—which I can either choose to detach myself from or choose to let get in the way of my performance.

When my ego starts talking smack like this, I mentally say the words *I am not these thoughts.* This powerful action shuts my ego down and then, nine times out of ten, I perform like a pro.

## The Peacemaker

When you stop listening to the voice in your head that compares you with others, holds grudges, and harbors resentments, your relationships are bound to improve.

Let me give you an example of a relationship that went from sucky to dope once I stopped listening to my ego. For about two years, I held a grudge against my cousin Al. We'd always been close, but then a stupid argument about a bird turned into a crazy fight. I'd found a bird in his yard that I wanted to keep and he wanted to sell. (It was an African Grey parrot, and I thought it was pretty cool. It talked, it flew to me when I called it, plus I'm just a lunatic animal lover.) I thought I was in the right because I found it. He thought he was in the right because it was his yard. Like I said, it was a stupid fight. Anyway, the fight got so serious he revoked his invitation for me to be godfather to his son. I was beyond pissed!

When I returned home after filming season 1 of *Jersey Shore,* I was in a real bad place mentally, and I couldn't take on any extra drama in my life. I'd been knocked down pretty hard; I already had all I could handle. This is when I turned down the voice of my bitchy ego and pushed all personal resentments aside. I knew this was an important step for me to take if I wanted to feel better. I made up with Al, and now he's one of my best friends. Understand this: making amends and saying "I'm sorry" doesn't make you the weaker person. It takes a real strong person to forgive, and the benefit is that it frees you from the voice in your head that holds draining and destructive grudges. Once you're free of those types of thoughts, all that's left is love and compassion. With that, your relationships get a positive bump.

## The Drama-Free Queen

When you're tapped in to your chill inner power, you'll find that you can interact with toxic people without getting sucked into their drama. In my line of work, this comes in handy a lot. I've been in situations where the drama-o-meter is dialed up high, but as long as I'm connected to the cool, calm, steady inside me, negativity cannot touch or hurt me. People can be screaming spiteful, hateful words all around me, and it doesn't matter so long as I stay insulated in my own little chill bubble. This is how I so often play the drama-free guido on *Jersey Shore.* When all hell breaks loose, I disconnect from my combative ego and tap in to my inner power. This allows me to remain steady while all around me tempers flare. I imagine that I am the sky, while the thunderstorms are passing through.

## IN THE REAL WORLD: It's Really You Against You

Let's say that someone is bullying and bothering you, getting all up in your face and trying to start an argument. Your natural reaction might be to jump in and allow the situation to escalate, but understand that you have another option. When negative thoughts and emotions are triggered inside you, you have the choice to react or to stop negativity dead in its tracks.

How? As soon as you feel your heartbeat begin to quicken, your blood pressure rise, or the tension mount—take a moment and acknowledge what's happening inside you. This takes practice, but if I'm being pushed around by some kid and start to feel stressed and tense and think angry thoughts like *I hate this kid. I'd like to kick his ass,* I take a deep breath and call my ego out. I'll say to myself, *Here they come again—another string of stupid thoughts trying to take over my mind and actions.*

You see, in this kind of situation, the biggest bully isn't the guy who's just gotten up in my face, but the bully *inside me*—my ego, "The Douche Bag." In other words: the battle I'm fighting is really within myself. It's me against my own mind. I can either let negative thoughts take me over and push me into a fight, or connect to my chill inner power, which maintains control. The choice is mine.

## The Cool Guy

When you operate from your chill inner power, you become the person who brings positive vibes to the party—the person everyone wants to be around. Think about the last time you were in a social scene. There's always someone, or a group of people, who are infecting the room with toxic energy and spreading hate and gossip. Then there's the crew on the other side of the room who have no agenda other than to positively connect with others and have a good time. For example, even when fists are flying in the Seaside house, Pauly and I continue to crack jokes and make each other laugh. I know fists are fun to watch on TV, but given the choice, what group of kids do you want to hang around in real life? I rest my case.

Bottom line: when you're tapped into your inner power, the people around you feel it. They sense that you're someone who doesn't judge and criticize—that you're someone supportive and fun to be around—and this frees them up to relax and tap in to their own power. Everybody wins.

**HOLD UP**

## Tough Guy

Maybe you're someone who doesn't think it's cool to be chill. It's not your *thing*. You'd rather be the person who gets attention for stirring up mad drama. Maybe it's important for you to wear your emotions on your sleeve, even if it means butting heads. Perhaps the act of making your point and defending your position gives you a charge, like the buzz from a Jäger bomb. I know a lot of people like you. How you act and behave is your choice; I'm not going to preach. But let me ask you this: how's life working out for you?

When I let my combative ego run the show, things didn't work out so well for me. In fact, my crazy mind nearly broke me. Now that I've learned how to quiet my mad thoughts and tap into the cool, calm, and steady inside me, life has started working *for* me, rather than against me. When you're chill, good will come your way. When you're dramatic, crazy will show up at your door.

---

## The Connector

The ego loves to stir up feelings like insecurity, jealousy, anger, and resentment. None of these emotions helps you to feel connected to other people. Take it from me—believing that you're all alone and against the world can, and most probably *will,* escalate any feelings of anxiousness or stress that are already at work inside you. My d-bag ego is a master at making me believe that I'm different and separate from everyone around me. When I'm at my lowest, I feel like no one gets me, and I put up a protective wall that puts distance between me and everyone in my life. I create my own loneliness. This is when it's especially important for me to remember that I am not my crazy, lonely thoughts. I am not alone! Underneath my Nike hoodie, I'm made of the same stuff as everyone else: pure positive energy and light. And if we're all made of the same stuff—no better, no worse—then we're all connected, and feelings like insecurity, jealousy, anger, resentment, and isolation have no place. Thoughts of separateness don't serve me or you, and also, they're not true.

## The Artist

With your ego shut down, you often do your best creative work. I like to draw. I've been drawing since I can remember. I'm a great copycat artist. I can copy anything, from a comic book to a picture of someone, and make it look like the original, and I've discovered that it's only when I've disconnected from my ego, which loves to overanalyze and judge, that I can really get into my artistic zone. Before joining *Jersey Shore,* I did murals for people's businesses. One time, I drew a genie on a huge wall for a hookah bar. I sat there for hours at a time quietly drawing. The world could have been collapsing around me, and it wouldn't have broken my concentration. I was tapped into my inner power and creating art. Life was good.

If you ask any great inventors, artists, or scientists about their greatest masterpieces and achievements, I bet they'd say that their best works came from somewhere else inside them. You see, your creative side is not inspired by your mind. Creativity is sparked when you're connected to *You,* your true power within.

## Mr. (and Ms.) Confident

When you put all these things together—heightened focus, kick-ass performance, chill relationships, positive vibes, a connection with other people, and amped-up creativity—your confidence gets a major boost. If you ask me, confidence is one of the most effective ways to stop the negative momentum of the mind. Confidence brings negativity to a screeching halt, and that's when your life starts to get better. When I walk into a club confidently, girls want me and guys want to be around me. When I walk into a pitch meeting confidently, people listen to what I have to say. And while impressing other people can be an important game-changer, the number one reason to be confident is for you. Confidence shuts down the ego and puts you positively back in control. When you're feeling strong and confident in yourself, negativity cannot touch *You.*

# Moving On ...

Understand that your ego does a fantastic job of blocking your connection to your inner power. Remember the 1999 cult classic *The Matrix,* where Neo, played by Keanu Reeves, realizes he has an important choice to make: he can stay trapped in a falsified dream world where he simply goes through the motions of life, or he can "wake up" to reality, where his true nature is more dynamic and powerful than he ever imagined. The choices aren't much different for you. In the next chapter, "Wake Up," you've got to decide—which way do you want to go? You can continue to be manipulated by your mind or wake up to the true *You* within.

# 3
# WAKE UP

**T**apping in to your inner power is never that far away. In fact, it's usually only *one thought* (or non-thought) away. What most people don't realize is that they have the power to disconnect from negative, sabotaging thoughts *at any time* by simply waking up to the present moment—the *right here, right now*. Once you "wake up," you gain access to your inner power, a positive force that'll help you beat back negativity before it has another chance to take you down.

In this chapter, "Wake Up," I'll tell you what I know about:

- Focusing on the *right here, right now*

- How to minimize distractions

- Tripping on the past and the future

- Playing it cool no matter what the situation

- Tuning in to the true *You*

## Right Here, Right Now

Before I tell you about my favorite tricks for waking up to the present moment, it's important that you understand exactly what "being present" means. To get the idea, when I was shooting season 4 of *Jersey Shore* in Florence, Italy, I discovered the Piazzale Michelangelo, which overlooks all of Florence. Every night, locals, students, and travelers all take a seat on its beautiful steps to get a front-row view of the sunset over the city. Imagine you're overlooking a chaotic city, and all of a sudden the flat light of day is transformed into dramatic oranges, pinks, and reds that change how everything looks and feels around you—I felt like I was bugging out. But I wasn't.

The Piazzale Michelangelo is awe inspiring, to say the least. It's crazy beautiful. The first time I stumbled across it, I was literally knocked out of my head and into the present moment. The colors of the sky, along with the fierce architecture and mad sounds of the city below, were so intense that they woke me up. In an instant, I forgot about all the drama that had been happening in the house and the fact that I was thousands of miles away from home. It's funny—when you wake up to the present moment, you forget your troubles, yet you're still intensely conscious. It's a pretty cool feeling.

The same thing would happen to me in the Piazza della Signoria, Florence's most famous square, right in the heart of the city. I'd sit there for hours at random cafés, ordering bangin' Italian meals and watching people from all over the world walk by. Every time I did this, it was like the little movie of my life suddenly started playing in an IMAX theater. Everything in the scene became bigger, louder, more colorful and intense. With so much going on around me, any thoughts that I might have been dwelling on magically disappeared. They no longer held my attention.

Can you relate to what I'm describing? Has something similar happened to you? Think back to a time when you were traveling or when you were on vacation and stumbled upon a dope piece of architecture, some sick artwork, or a plate of food that looked crazy good. Moments like these are examples of when we're wide awake, alert to the present—the right here, right now. You remember these moments, right? They feel different. You feel different, and that's because when you're focused on what's right in front of you in real time, your mind stops making noise, and you wake up to *You*.

**BREAK IT DOWN**

## The Right Here, Right Now

Some of my favorite spiritual and personal growth gurus refer to the *right here, right now* as "the present," "the now," and "the moment." However you want to label it, it's what's happening *right* in front of you in real time. When you're focused on it, any thoughts you might have been obsessing over magically disappear. When you "wake up," your mind stops making noise, and as Eckhart Tolle says, "living in the *now* is the truest path to happiness and enlightenment."

You see, your ego—the primary source of negative talk in your head—loses its voice in the present moment. When you're zoomed in on what's real, it's as if your ego comes down with a bad case of laryngitis. This is because the ego lives in the past and in the future. Think about it—what are your most nagging thoughts preoccupied with? Something that already happened, or something you fear is or isn't gonna happen. Am I right?

The ego lives in another time zone, which is why waking up to the moment works so well to shut down shitty feelings like sadness, regret, resentment, past hostility and grief, worry, dread, fear, and anxious anticipation about the future. When you're focused on the right here, right now, your ego has no power; it can't make a play. Game over, man. Game over! In fact, it's *only* in the immediate moment that you can effectively escape the negative voice in your head, which is why I've become such a huge fan of practicing this technique. On more than a few occasions, it's really saved me from losin' it!

Let me remind you that when I was in college, the voice in my head had gotten so cruel and unrelenting that I contemplated suicide—not because I really wanted to end my life, but because I thought suicide would be the fastest way to shut my mind up! Seriously, I was about to go to that extreme just to enjoy some peace and quiet. After learning that thoughts are just creations of the mind, I realized how free I could be if I simply disconnected from them. After trying several different tools, "waking up" to the present moment proved to be one of the fastest and most straightforward ways to shut my mind up!

## HOLD UP

## Anyone Can Wake Up

Just a quick reminder that you don't have to be someone who suffers from chronic anxiety like I do to benefit from the mental tricks I'm describing here. The practice of "waking up" will help you whoever you are and whatever your situation. For example, I'm sure you suffer from your share of bad days; you've likely been bullied by a negative thought that put you in a nasty mood. Most of us are ruled by our minds more than we think we are, and by learning how to focus on the moment and shut down the mind, we can rid our lives of a lot of stress and negativity. So even if you haven't fallen down the scary, dark rabbit hole like I have, arming yourself with this tool is still a smart move. At some point—and probably sooner than later—it'll come in handy.

---

## Minimize Distractions

Most of us have had moments when we feel wide awake and fully present to what's going on around us. Unfortunately, this clarity and heightened awareness doesn't usually stick with us for very long. Before we know it—BOOM—the mind noise returns, and our sweet little moment is over; once again, life is projected onto a small screen.

What if I told you that you could have those experiences in your ordinary, everyday life—at work or at school, at home and driving around your own neighborhood—and they would last longer than a few seconds? Are you into that?

You see, you don't have to be in a mind-blowing place like downtown Florence to temporarily escape from the noise in your own head. Nor do you have to go to extremes like signing up for skydiving lessons to feel alert to the right here, right now. A lot of people think that it takes something like jumping from a height of ten thousand feet to wake up to their lives—as in *Holy shit, I'm going to fall to my death—right now!* Such extremes are not necessary. A sick thrill, maybe, but not essential to snap you out of the past and the future and into the *now*.

You can wake up to the moment at any time by simply minimizing the distractions around you. This is how you can experience the high of life I'm talking about every day. To be fair, this is easier said than done because distractions are everywhere. In today's tech-obsessed culture, we're surrounded by them—TV, iPod, iPad, BlackBerry, and don't even get me started on social media like Facebook, Tumblr, and Twitter that dominate our time and attention. I'm not saying that technology is *bad*. I'm a huge fan of it. The Internet is amazing. Anything and everything you want to know about is available to you, at any time. And social media are a lot of fun. I love connecting with my fans and cracking jokes on Twitter, and BBM'ing or texting can be super efficient for making last-minute plans and getting in touch with people immediately. I have all the newest techy gadgets, and I use them all (the Flip cam is my latest obsession. I'm always filming funny things and posting them online). That said, I'm mindful of how I let them use *me*. You see, when you engage in round-the-clock technology, you're unconsciously training your mind to be somewhere *other* than the present moment, and when you allow your mind and thoughts to wander like this, you fall prey to anxiousness, stress, and a mixed bag of other negative thoughts and emotions.

## Mind Rides

Not sure you get it? Let me give you an example. Say you BBM some guy you want to hook up with. Whether you're aware of it or not, as soon as you send that message, your mind goes somewhere else; it abandons the present moment. Maybe you start wondering where he'll be when he gets your message, how he'll respond, or what he might say to his homies about you. With your mind in this other place, you lose touch with your immediate surroundings, and when you cut yourself off from what's going on right in front of you, you invite stress into your life. Truth! You might not feel it immediately, but by checking out and preoccupying yourself with *what might be,* you open the door to mental anxiety.

And what really sucks about living in another time zone: your physical body reacts to wherever your mind is too. I mentioned this earlier, and the situation I've just described is a perfect example of how it plays out: mental anxiety, be it frustration, fear, dread, or worry over how some kid might respond to your hot and heavy sext, will create physical stress in your body. If you think, *He must not be into me because he didn't text me back right* away—*I'll probably never hear from him again*, you may feel edgy, uneasy, and like you want to throw up. But here's the thing—you don't actually *know* that he's not into you. The rejection you've created in your mind isn't real. You've simply imagined an outcome that may or may not prove to be true; you've let your mind take you for a ride, and as a result, you emotionally and physically suffer for it. If only you'd stayed present after pressing Send, you could have avoided all that unnecessary stress.

Hear me out—I'm not suggesting that you stop using your phone, computer, or whatever else. Just become aware of how your favorite toys propel you out of the present moment. I'd bet that most people spend less than 20 percent of their time focused on what's going on right in front of them (and even less if they're hard-core gamers). Ask yourself, *How long can I sit still without checking my phone for new texts, tweets, messages, or e-mails?* I'll be honest—this is a major challenge for me and most everyone I know. I probably check my Twitter feed every three to four minutes. If I'm not careful to stay connected to who I'm with or where I am, I can easily get lost in outer space. Bye-bye Vinny.

## IN THE REAL WORLD: Modern-Day Slavery

Indulge in technology—just don't become a slave to it. Trust me, I know it's a good escape mechanism, but it also has the power to stress you out. If you notice you're becoming totally preoccupied with getting messages on your phone, or if you're getting all worked up and upset over something someone is saying about you online, try shutting the computer off, putting down the phone, and walking outside to get some air. I get nasty, hateful comments almost every day on my social media pages. I have to make a concentrated effort not to get sucked in. One way I do this is by putting tools to work that help me reconnect with the present moment—that is, with what's *real,* not what's behind a computer screen or a cell phone. If you do this, you can freely use technology without its making you a slave.

When we're on the set of *Jersey Shore,* the entire cast is cut off from any access to the Internet, television, radio, and our laptops and phones. (These are standard reality TV rules, by the way.) This is always a shock at first. All of us on the show seem to go through an initial withdrawal period, but after a couple of days, I actually feel okay without all my techie toys. For example, I'll stick my hand in my pocket, and when my phone's not there, instead of freaking out, I realize that I really don't need it or miss it. Imagine that—I don't *need* my phone to survive. What a concept. In fact, I feel a whole lot less anxious without its distracting my attention and pulling me away from what I'm doing in the present moment.

While there are distractions around us all the time, you do have the power to "wake up" anytime, anywhere, when you have the *right tools,* and that's what my program is all about. Below, I introduce you to one of my all-time favorite mental workouts for waking up. I borrowed it from Eckhart Tolle and Wayne W. Dyer and gave it my own twist. Give it a try.

## VINNY'S MENTAL WORKOUT

## Listen Between the Lines

We're conditioned to listen to the sounds around us—conversations, traffic on the street, dogs barking, babies crying, the alarm clock beeping, whatever. A great trick for waking yourself up to the *right here, right now* is to turn your focus away from the sounds around you and instead focus on the silence *in between* the noise. For example, say you're out to dinner and there are conversations going on all around you. Instead of tuning in to what people are saying, try tuning in to the silent pauses between their words. It may sound like a weird thing to do but give it a try. Once you've gotten the hang of tuning in to the silence in between other people's words, try it on *yourself.*

Close your eyes and tune in to your ego—the nonstop nagging voice in your head. What is it worrying about today? Work? Family? Money? A recent breakup? The ten pounds you want to lose? Whatever your thoughts are, let them flow uninterrupted for a few minutes.

Now direct your attention to the silent pauses in between those thoughts. When one thought ends, there's probably a pause before the next thought starts. Focus on those pauses—the silence in between the noise. Listen to what *isn't* there versus what *is* there. Catch my drift?

When you focus on the silence, your mind goes silent. Congratulations—you've just shut down your ego and woken up to the present moment. Feelings of anxiousness, stress, and general negativity should have all but disappeared!

When you first start playing around with this exercise, you might notice that the pauses in between your thoughts are infrequent at best. No problem. This is completely normal. Thoughts have a tendency to piggyback on top of one another. You might also notice that holding your focus on the silent pauses in between your thoughts is a major challenge. Again—very normal. When the silence is interrupted by your noisy mind, simply wait for the next break in conversation, and refocus your attention on the silence between your thoughts. As you continue to do this mental workout, set a goal to focus longer on the pauses between your thoughts and to spend less time listening to the nonstop talking and anxiousness created by your mind. You will find that as you do this, the silent pauses s-t-r-e-t-c-h, and you'll feel a lot more chill, peaceful, and calm.

The workout I've just walked you through can be a tough one to get a handle on, but it's worth the effort because it's super power-ful. Some of my favorite spiritual teachers refer to it as drawing the distinction between *thinking* your thoughts and *listening* to your thoughts. Believe it or not, there's actually a big difference between the two. Let me explain: *Thinking* your thoughts is automatic. It's what most of us do. Thoughts pop in and out of our heads. We let them flow uninterrupted, and as a general rule we accept them without question. When you *listen* to your thoughts you become conscious of them, which allows you to question them, disassociate from them, and break any emotional attachment to them. When you listen to your thoughts it's kinda like you're listening in on a conversation that someone else is having. In fact, that's exactly what you're doing. You're listening to your ego—the voice that's separate from *You*. As soon as you start listening to your thoughts, you acknowledge that your thoughts are just crazy creations of your mind; they're not really *You*. Get it?

## Do You

As soon as you wake up to the *right here, right now,* the calmer and less anxious you'll feel. That's when you'll know you've successfully gotten out of your head and you're simply *being*, rather than thinking. That's freedom! And when you're free of all the garbage in your head—guess what? You're back in control of your life. Once you wake up to the present moment, madness could be breaking loose all around you—in my case, the mad drunken drama of housemates calling one another names—and you remain the steadiest guy in the room. How's this? Because once you silence the mind and become present, you start to feel the *presence* of your cool, calm, and steady inner power. And remember, this power is available to you at all times because it exists in you. It *is You*. Your thoughts come and go, while your inner power is always there, just beneath the surface like the deep ocean floor.

Want to give it a try? On the next page is another mental workout to help quiet your mind and wake you up to *You*!

# Become Mindful

Pick a simple activity you enjoy doing: taking a walk, listening to music, working out at the gym, making dinner for friends. It really doesn't matter what you do, as long as you're completely alert and focused on whatever it is. Many spiritual teachers and personal growth gurus call this the act of being "mindful." You can be mindful in whatever you do, and when you are—you *wake up*.

I regularly practice mindfulness in a number of ways, but one of my favorite times to do it is when I draw. I do my best artistic work when I'm totally focused on nothing other than my pencils and paper and my "thinking" mind is shut down. I also practice mindfulness when I walk or run by counting my steps as I go and focusing on what the ground feels like underneath my feet. You can make any activity mindful from doing a set of ten sit-ups to drinking (and tasting!) a cold glass of water. Another way I practice mindfulness is while reading. A book with a great story that really sucks me in helps me to stay mindful. You can be mindful when watching your favorite TV show by really focusing on the characters and how the plot plays out. (Watching TV is *not* a mindful activity if you use it as background noise while doing or thinking about other things.) Same thing goes with music. When listening to your favorite songs, instead of letting them transport you to another time zone, really concentrate on the words and what they mean to you today. And if none of those activities works to quiet your noisy mind, become mindful of your breath. Like I mentioned before, breathing is one of my favorite quick-fix tricks for quieting the mind.

Begin to practice mindfulness to wake yourself up to what's going on right in front of you in real time. If you start to lose yourself in your mind, bring your attention back to what you're doing. Do this until your thoughts fall away and your mind goes blank. Once you've stopped thinking, sense the calm, cool presence inside *You*.

## Use Your Mind—Don't Let It Use You

Not sure you get the whole "not-thinking" thing? No problem. Thinking about not thinking can be confusing. Let me try to explain it another way—turning off your mind is not the same thing as not thinking. You still need to use your mind to make decisions, solve problems, figure things out—and basically function day to day. I would've gotten completely lost walking around Florence during season 4 of *Jersey Shore* if I hadn't been relying on my brain to read a map. (And even still, I had a hard time finding my way around, although I wasn't as challenged as some of my roommates.) Without a doubt—the mind is useful. I'm not encouraging you to become a walking zombie. I'm simply suggesting that you turn off the compulsive, nonstop stream of negative thoughts that (a) keep you stuck in the past or focused on the future and (b) trigger negative emotions that trigger negative behaviors. In other words, this practice is about learning to use your mind instead of letting it use *you*.

By getting a handle on your thoughts, you take back control of your emotions, reactions, and interactions. In fact, once you learn to quiet the noise in your head, you may be surprised to discover how much faster and more efficiently your brain works. It's ironic, but remember what I said in the last chapter—with the garbage out of the way, you'll likely become more alert, aware, and focused. Not to mention, experience and feel things more intensely. Waking up to the present moment is like a drug high, except it's free and doesn't wreck your life.

I can't begin to tell you how many times getting out of my head has given me a powerful advantage. When we're filming *Jersey Shore*, for example, and mad drama is heating up all around me (a certain boyfriend and girlfriend are in the middle of a five-hour fight), I can almost always find a way to shut down my mind, "wake up," and connect with my inner power—the steady cool within me. This puts me back in control and allows me to keep an even head when two full-on angry chicks are going at it and trying to drag me into the middle of a catfight. As long as I stay present and don't get lost in *my* head, nine times out of ten I can remain chill and walk away without so much as a scratch.

## HOLD UP

## Not a Drama-Free Guarantee

Waking up to the right here, right now doesn't guarantee that things will always go well. Sometimes crazy shit is unavoidable, and you have to get out of the ring—that is, physically remove yourself from a situation before it gets worse. During the taping of season 5 of *Jersey Shore,* my overthinking mind and chronic anxiety returned with a vengeance. I was suffering from nonstop headaches and night sweats. Add to that, I lost my appetite, started to drop weight, and developed a nasty cough that wouldn't go away. I felt awful. I looked awful. While my roommates totaled it up to "Vinny's in a funk," I knew it was more serious than that. I started using every tool at my disposal to pull myself out of my dark place, but I was stuck. After several days, I did what I had to do. I bailed. I physically removed myself from the show. I went home, where I was able to recharge and reconnect with my inner power, and then when I was ready, I returned to Seaside—calm, cool, and back in control.

---

I practice the technique of snapping "awake" not only when I'm on the set, but also when I have an important meeting or when I'm doing a live interview. In these kinds of situations, I make sure to walk into the room at a zero ego level—meaning, I get out of my head. As soon as whoever I'm talking to recognizes that I'm fully present, he or she will often join me on my level, and before you know it, we're having a real conversation free of bullshit.

It took me some time to get this technique down, so be patient as you practice it yourself. It's not an easy thing to do. No less than three years ago, I used to walk into random meetings and job interviews all nervous and sweaty, expecting the worst. Back then, my anxious and fearful mind was in crazy control, so I naturally assumed that at any moment, something would go wrong and the meeting would blow up in my face. After I began practicing my program, however, I realized that my nerves were just a response to my negative thoughts. If I could kill the thoughts, I could kill the nerves. As long as I checked my ego at the door *before* walking into the room, I was a lot more confident and in control during the meeting.

That's not to say that feelings of anxiousness wouldn't come up; they did and still do. But what's different today is how I deal with those thoughts and feelings. No matter how tense or contentious the situation, I know that I always have the tools to disconnect from my crazy thoughts and tap into my inner power. As long as I do this, I can get through any meeting, interview, or public speech, no problem.

# IN THE REAL WORLD: Bring Your Lucky Charm

Knowing how to tune in to the right here, right now is like carrying around a lucky charm. (In fact, you may consider carrying some kind of charm around with you that you can rub or touch throughout the day to remind you of all the new tools you're learning. I wear my grandfather Sal's gold chain, which he left me when he died.) I certainly never leave home without it when I want to meet girls.

When I go to a club, for example, I put this tool to work as soon as I walk in the door. How? By acting like a dog. That might sound silly, but hear me out—dogs are the perfect role models because dogs don't think! They live in the moment. They have no ego. They don't judge. They're cool and calm and give off a nonthreatening vibe. (You think I'm crazy? Trust me, you can learn a lot from observing a dog. Jelly, my English bulldog, who recently passed away, was one of my greatest teachers.)

Most girls know when they're being faked, so when I enter a club, I check my ego at the door and focus on being completely present with whoever I'm talking to. When she's talking—I don't look behind her— I'm into *her*. I'm present, and this draws girls in. I don't like to make a habit of bragging, but when I'm awake to the right here, right now, and fully myself, I kill it with the girls.

*Note:* I may act like a dog, but not in a disrespectful kind of way. I have huge respect for the women I spend time with. All I'm saying here is that when you curb your ego and let your true self off leash, you will attract people to *You*.

# Really Now

What if I told you that the past and the future don't exist and that the present—what's going on right in front of you right now—is the only *real* thing? Sure, situations in the past happened, and more events will unfold in the future, but what's truly real is what's happening *today*. Right now, in the present moment. People, in general, have a hard time getting this. To borrow from Eckhart Tolle, if you asked a dog on the street what time it was, he'd look at you sideways and say, "Bro, what are you talking about? The time is right now." Animals live in the moment, while their thickheaded owners live in a number of different time zones—the past and the future, predominantly. Why do we do this? Why are we constantly stuck in a mental time machine?

We cling to the past because we rely on our past experiences, challenges, struggles, and achievements to define who we are today. We wear our past around like a coat on our back. Remember that social costume I talked about in the last chapter? Many of us let our past experiences influence the social costume we wear today. For example, in my bedroom in Staten Island, I have a Sicilian flag hanging on my wall alongside sports awards I won as a kid, my bachelor's degree from CUNY College of Staten Island, and random artwork I've done over the years. All this stuff from the past identifies me; it reminds me who "Vinny Guadagnino" is—the reality star, the athlete, the artist, the college-educated kid—and while all this stuff provides me with a sense of safety and comfort, the truth is, I don't really need any of it to reassure me of who I am. Underneath my social costume, I'm just like you—pure light and energy—a powerful force that exists in the present moment. The past happened, and it holds significance, but it's gone. It's over. Yet I'm still here. Who I am is who I am *right now*. Get it?

## Thinking Won't Get You There

Just a reminder—be patient with yourself if what I'm describing isn't immediately clear. The key to "getting" any of these concepts is to experience them, rather than overthink them (I know, easier said than done). Whenever I get frustrated, I affirm to myself by saying out loud, "This cannot be comprehended by my mind." Take your time. It's not a race, and in fact, you've probably covered more distance than you think you have since opening the first page of this book. Give it time to sink in.

As for why our minds like to fast-forward into the future—many of us have convinced ourselves that the good stuff is just up ahead. In a week, a month, or a year, more money, success, fame, or the right girl or guy awaits us. So long as we hold out, we'll find our happiness.

Do you really think that's true? Is the future going to be that much better than today? How can you be so sure? What makes you so convinced that if you can't enjoy your life right now, you'd enjoy tomorrow or the day after any better?

What if I told you that the only thing you can truly count on is the life you're living *this very moment*. Does that bum you out? It shouldn't. Instead of regarding the present moment as a meaningless cab ride to some imaginary destination—face it, the future you envision may never come, and if it does, you'll more than likely create a "new" and "better" future in your mind to start longing for—understand that you *do* have the power to create more success, fame, security, and happiness in the present moment. In fact, that's the only place you can create positive change, because the right here, right now is the only thing you have any control over.

## IN THE REAL WORLD: Take Action, Son!

Do you often dwell on past situations and think about how you would have done things differently? Maybe even over and over again? Do you regularly imagine future scenarios or "mental movies" that create anxiety, frustration, or worry for you—imaginary scenes that you spend way too much time trying to solve, or *stop,* before they happen? How's that working out for you? I bet that if you could charge admission to all the mental movies your mind has dreamt up, you'd make a killing! My advice? Stop wasting your time. If you want more control in your life, get out of the mental time machine and take action *today*! The present moment is the only situation you have any control over. Let the past and the future GO!

I don't like to fly, which has turned out to be very inconvenient. When I'm not shooting, I'm often on a plane two or three times a week. If I don't keep my thoughts in check, I can easily work myself into an anxiety attack before I even start to pack. If I do start to flip out, I just hit the pause button: I tell myself that my fear of crashing and burning is just a reaction to a mental movie my mind has created about a future that *doesn't even exist.* Therefore there's nothing to prevent or control. *Let it go, Vinny.* Trying to fix past situations or control future outcomes will only make you crazy, because you simply cannot control something that's already happened or hasn't happened yet. On the other hand, you have absolute control over your actions and reactions *in the present*. If a problem arises, accept it or deal with it—and move on. It's really that simple. While you have no control over the past or the future, you have insane power in the right here, right now.

## IN THE REAL WORLD: Deal with It Head-On

As a little kid, I'd often get dragged into street fights with other neighborhood kids. These fights were relatively harmless, and yet I remember always being mad nervous "the day of the fight" when other kids on my street ran around advertising it. However, as soon as the fight got under way, and we were rolling around kicking and slapping one another, my nerves disappeared. Who has time to be scared when you're focusing on your next bitch move?

This is a silly example; my point is that when you're faced with a legit problem you have to immediately deal with, you just deal with it. There's really no time to overthink it and freak out. Freaking out happens *ahead of time,* when you dwell on what *might happen,* and this mental movie isn't real—it's just a creation of your crazy mind. Turn off the projector and deal with your problems head-on, and I bet you'll discover that you can handle whatever's thrown your way just fine.

When my cousin Doug, who is almost always positive and present, loses touch with this message, he immediately starts complaining about his life. He will call me five days a week bitching about every miserable aspect of his whack job. He'll say things like "If I had *this* job . . . if I had *that* job . . . my life would be better." I have to remind him that instead of complaining, he should do something about it. "Take action, son," I say. "Get on the computer and start filling out applications *today*. You have the capability to fill out at least ten today if you put your mind to it. Start with one! By the end of the month, I bet you'll have at least five interviews lined up, and one of those five might lead to a better job."

Understand that the present moment is where your life is happening. It'll never happen at any other time. When you spend the majority of your hours waiting on the future for fulfillment or lingering in the past, you only create more anxiousness, worry, and stress in your life. Wake up to your life today. It's the only real thing.

## My Religion

I'm so into this concept that I like to say that while I was raised Catholic, the religion I currently follow is the present moment. The right here, right now allows us to access our inner power—our cool, calm, and steady self. When we're present, we're happier and healthier people, and we're able to make connections with people that are *real*. In a world full of haters and posers, it's not often easy to feel connected to others. I certainly used to feel that way. But once I learned how to disconnect from my negative thoughts and enjoy the serenity of a quiet mind, I finally understood how we're all connected.

Did you see the 2009 epic sci-fi film *Avatar*? Director James Cameron created a fictional world called Pandora, where its native inhabitants, the Na'vi, are spiritually interconnected with one another and, likewise, connected to the mother-goddess Eywa (Life, the Source, the Universe) through the mystical Tree of Souls. When I saw this movie, I couldn't help but see the similarities between

Cameron's fictional world and my understanding of how we're interconnected on Earth. What I believe is that we're all connected by the present moment. I believe the present not only connects us with one another but also links us to the source of our inner power. For lack of a better word, I'll call this God.

I don't want to get too deep and heavy into a discussion on religion, but I think it's worth mentioning that when I was in college and my depression was at its worst, I felt like God had abandoned me. This was a terrifying, powerless, and very confusing time in my life. I was haunted by the idea that the God I'd prayed to my whole life had up and left my side. It was only later that I realized that God had not abandoned me. God was with me all along. In the present moment. Inside me. *As me*. As pure, positive light and love. And isn't that what real faith is all about?

**HOLD UP**

## Did Vinny Really Just Go There?

If my dropping the "God" card turns you off or freaks you out, chill. I'm not preaching. You don't have to be religious to wake up to your life right now. The tools to do so are available to anyone who wants to use them. Your religion has nothing to do with it.

## All Day Every Day

Now that you understand what being "awake" means, I encourage you to get into the practice of waking up every day—and I'm not talking about getting out of bed. I'm referring to being mindful and living in the present moment. Treat this practice like a workout. I used to sell gym memberships, and our biggest selling point was "You don't have time NOT to work out." Well, you don't have time *not* to work out your mind either.

Every day, become aware of how rarely your attention is spent in the right here, right now. Believe it or not, simply becoming aware that you aren't present actually helps snap you awake. So awareness of your unawareness is a positive first step.

Set a goal to quiet your mind for some amount of time every day. This doesn't have to be a huge time commitment, so relax. You could spend as little as one to five minutes practicing one of my earlier mental workouts—"Listen Between the Lines" (page 79) or "Become Mindful" (page 82). As you continue your practice in the days and weeks ahead, try withdrawing your attention from the past and the future, and instead try focusing on the right here, right now for longer stretches of time.

Monitor your reactions to the people and situations around you to gauge if you're operating from your ego or your true self. If emotions like fear, insecurity, defensiveness, or frustration are triggered by something someone around you says or does, this is a strong indicator that you're stuck in your head and not focused on the moment.

VINNY'S MENTAL WORKOUT

## Rate It on the Negativity-o-Meter

The key is to get a handle on your thoughts *before* they take you for a ride. For this purpose, I've created the Negativity-o-Meter. Get into a daily habit of asking yourself, *How am I feeling?* On a scale of 1 to 5, rate your level of negativity—frustration, tension, anxiety, sadness, insecurity, fear—where 5 is "I'm in a dark place" and 1 is "I'm feeling pretty peaceful and chill." Just rating your negativity will help you get present, because this practice alone forces you to separate from your thoughts.

If you notice that your mind thoughts are amped up and your negativity level has crept past a 2, try to determine what thoughts triggered a negative reaction. Ask yourself, *What thoughts are setting me off? Am I stuck in the past? Trying to control the future?* Remember, your emotions are triggered by your thoughts. You can trace any emotion you have back to its original thought. This takes practice, but your awareness will build over time—and with it, your ability to shut down your mind and "wake up" to the present moment will strengthen as well.

Your goal is to stay in a Zen place so you never get to a crazy place. You feel me? Becoming present sends any wave of negativity rippling backward. It's like a tsunami in reverse. Once you're free of your crazy mind thoughts, you can easily operate from your inner power.

## Moving On . . .

Okay, time to take a mental break. For a program focused on the power of quieting the mind, we've spent almost half of this book stuck in our heads, so let's shift gears. In the next chapter, "Hit the Gym," I'll explain how high-energy physical activities can also wake *You* up and connect you to your inner power.

BODY

# 4
# HIT THE GYM

Getting a handle on your thoughts doesn't require just a mental workout. Negative thinking can, and should, be attacked on a physical level, as well. From playing a pickup game of basketball in the park to stretching my body like saltwater taffy in a yoga class, I've found that moving my body helps snap me out of my head and usually reduces my anxiety and improves my overall mood.

In this chapter, "Hit the Gym," I'll tell you what I know about:

- How your physical health is directly related to your mental health

- Developing a workout routine that works best for you

- The importance of getting your Z's

- How to jump back into the program *if* you've slacked off

Boiled down to one phrase, it's simple: if I don't feel good physically, I'm not going to feel good mentally. Sure, I work out for cosmetic reasons too. I want to look good so that I can throw my swagfit the next time I'm walking the red carpet. But for me, the biggest benefit of staying fit and working out is that it helps me to stay chill.

You've already heard me talk about how negative thoughts trigger negative emotions that can often manifest as physical pain, stress, and tension in your body. I've personally experienced this A + B = C scenario more times than I'd like to remember. There was a point during my first semester at SUNY New Paltz, for example, when my nerves were so out of whack that every time I ate, my cheeks would swell up. And because I also wasn't getting enough sleep during this time, my eyes would twitch. As if feeling miserable on the inside wasn't bad enough, I looked like a strung-out chipmunk.

On the set of *Jersey Shore,* there have been many times when, in an effort to appear "normal," I've had to hide the outward signs of my anxiety from my roommates and the camera crew. If my hands are sweaty, for example, I shove them in my pockets. If I start to feel dizzy, I sit down. If I have a stress headache, I grin and bear it. Of course, none of these sleight-of-hand coping tricks ever relieves the real problem. Thankfully, I've found something that does. I simply *redirect* the physical manifestation of my anxiety into high-intensity exercise. In other words, I work my anxiety *out* before it works me *over.*

I've discovered that regular exercise is one of the best ways to relieve a stress headache, an anxious stomach, a racy heart, tense shoulders, and pent-up negative energy. Even better, I've found that physical exercise not only redirects negativity out of my body, it helps to prevent it from entering my system in the first place!

The direct connection between getting regular physical exercise and stress release—in addition to alleviating more serious conditions like chronic anxiety and depression—isn't just personal to me. The research proves it. According to the Mayo Clinic, physical exercise has been found to help manage and ease shitty, anxious feelings and generally enhance one's mood in a number of ways. Here's how:

1. Exercise releases feel-good endorphins, making you feel naturally high and pumped up.

2. It *reduces* other brain chemicals and hormones like cortisol that can intensify negative feelings.

3. It boosts your total body temperature, which can have a calming effect on your mind.

4. It forces you to breathe, which also helps calm the mind.

5. It makes you stronger, it makes you look better, and it makes you feel more confident. Triple win.

Some studies have even suggested that regular, high-intensity physical exercise may work as well as, if not better than, some prescribed medications for improving your feel-good mood and combating more serious conditions like depression. Since I'm a big fan of natural remedies, coming across this research has felt especially empowering to me.

In addition to the chemical effect on your mood, physical exercise also serves as a great distraction. When you're focused on moving, stretching, and pushing your body to the limit, you're less likely to be fixated on what's going on in your head. Physical exercise helps to shut down the mind and wake you up to the right here, right now, where you can tap into your inner power. And you know me—I'm always looking for quick-fix tools that can accomplish this goal.

Want to give it a try? Jump in with this simple workout to quiet your mind and wake you up to the cool, calm, and steady *You*.

## Find Your Pulse

Pick a physical activity that will spike your heart rate in under five minutes. Jog or walk quickly around the block, take the stairs in your office building, drop and do five or ten push-ups or a series of squat jumps. It really doesn't matter what you do, as long as it gets your heart pumping fairly quickly and noticeably.

Once you feel the blood flowing, sit down somewhere comfortable and focus your attention on either the beating of your heart or the rise and fall of your breath. Anchor yourself in your body, and concentrate only on your heart pumping blood and your lungs taking in air.

Body awareness gets you out of your head and helps to wake you up to the right here, right now—the source of your inner power.

If you start to lose yourself in your mind, bring your attention back to your pulse and breath. Do this until your thoughts fall away and your mind goes blank. Once you've stopped thinking, sense the calm, cool presence inside *You*—that's your *inner power*.

## Create a Routine

So now that you've gotten a taste of how physical exercise can get you out of your head, temporarily releasing feelings of anxiety, stress, and general negativity, create a physical workout that you can fold into your daily life.

When I was finishing out my poli-sci degree at CUNY Staten Island, I worked as a personal trainer at Bally Total Fitness, and that's where I created a personal routine that balances high-intensity cardio, strength conditioning, and flexibility. This is the routine I still follow today. You too should create an exercise routine that consists of activities you like to do—otherwise you won't do it.

## Pick Up the Pace

If you watch *Jersey Shore,* you know my current lifestyle involves regularly hitting the gym. But unlike some gym rats, I'm not motivated by stationary exercise machines like a treadmill or an elliptical. I'm more likely to jump into a basketball game than onto a StairMaster. I've always been involved in some kind of competitive sport—baseball, track, swimming, tennis, football, with basketball at the top of the list. So as a general rule, I try to make sure every gym I join or visit has a court.

Playing basketball is my all-time favorite way to get a high-intensity workout. If I had my way, I'd play ball every day of the week. When my schedule allows, I run around the court Monday through Friday for at least an hour at a time. Now sometimes I simply can't fit it in, but that's what I aim for—a solid hour of high-intensity cardio three to five days a week.

A vigorous physical activity like basketball gets my heart pumping and my blood flowing. In my opinion, it's better than any energy shot you can find on the market, plus it's natural and free. In addition to giving me a positive energy boost, a game like basketball forces me to focus on the right here, right now and is one of the best remedies I've found for my anxious and negative thoughts. After an intense pickup game, my focus is clearer, my mood is better, and any emotional baggage that I might have brought onto the court is generally gone. My game mantra: leave the bullshit on the court.

In Seaside, I'm undefeated in pickup games on the basketball court. Even when I've been at my worst, consumed with feelings of mad dread, I've played basketball because I know getting into a game will help me mentally. At my lowest moments, you'll find me at the gym challenging people to a game. With my mind focused on beating my opponent, I'm less focused on how miserable I feel.

As an added benefit, playing competitive sports like basketball is a social activity, and doctors will tell you that interacting with other people also serves as a great mental distraction. When you're engaged with other people, you can't focus as intently on yourself and the wild thoughts running round your mind.

When I can't play basketball, I run—often at two or three in the morning, when the streets are quiet, dark, and empty. Running has an immediate calming effect on me. Especially if there's a nice, cool breeze. It's like my tension and worries are simply lifted and carried away. I feel so present during those moments. It's just me, the silence of the night, the stars, and the ground underneath my feet. Running is a great activity for practicing mindfulness; you can focus on your lungs filling up and pushing out air, or your feet hitting the ground one step at a time.

Completing a three- to five-mile run before the sun has even had a chance to come up gives me a positive jump start on the day. It "wakes" me up and connects me to my cool, calm, and steady inner power. After an early morning run and a hot shower, I feel like I can accomplish just about anything. It's dope.

# Getting High

To best combat anxiety, stress, and tension, doctors recommend an exercise routine that includes some amount of high-intensity cardio. I like to run and play basketball. What do you like to do? Find an activity that you like that'll get your heart pumping, your blood flowing, and your sweat glands working overtime, and then integrate it into your regular workout. I know a lot of people who swear by Tony Horton's *P90X Extreme Home Fitness* DVDs. (I do this in my boxers sometimes when I'm on the road. You would die laughing if you saw it.)

*A word of caution:* Too much cardio can cause a tension headache and other feelings of stress in the body, so exercise in moderation. Do what feels right.

---

## Pick Up the Weights

I balance out my cardio workout with strength conditioning. The days I'm able to make it to the gym, I spend an hour on the court and an hour in the weight room. I like to keep my workouts interesting, so I mix up my weight routine by focusing on different muscle groups on different days. Over the course of a week, I'll hit every major muscle group until I burn them all out, and then I'll start the cycle all over again. In my experience, if your routine bores you, you won't be motivated to work hard, which is why I'm constantly changing it up.

While lifting weights doesn't get my heart pumping as much as running around a basketball court, it does require me to focus my attention on the present moment. When I'm doing shoulder presses with sixty-pound weights, it's pretty hard to think about anything else. If I do, I may lose my grip and drop the bar on my chest—and then I'm *really* hating life. Lifting weights works wonders to quiet my mind and connect me to my cool, calm, and clear self. It's a win.

## IN THE REAL WORLD: Leave the Excuses at Home

You know you should work out, but if you're feeling low, dragging your butt to the gym might be the last thing you want to do. It's easier to stay in your pajamas or sweats all day. I get it. Sometimes I have a hard time motivating myself to leave the house. I'd rather take a nap or zone out in front of the TV. And if I have a hangover, forget it! In these situations, I literally have to force myself into my gym clothes and into the car. And while I might spend the entire ride bitching and moaning—*This is a waste of time . . . I feel terrible . . . I really don't want to be doing this*—as soon as I walk into the gym, I'm glad to be there. Why? Because I always feel better afterwards. Always. So if you find yourself wrestling with the question, *Should I work out or take a nap?*, the answer is—WORK OUT. You'll be glad you did.

### Stretch It Out

I'm often the only twenty-four-year-old guy in yoga class at my gym on Staten Island, the Shore, wherever, and I'll be honest—when I first started going, I felt pretty awkward. I wandered in one day off the basketball court all sweaty and stinky in a tank top and shorts and quickly realized I had to remove my sneakers and socks if I wanted to stay. I thought about turning around and walking right back out the door, but at the time, I was feeling particularly anxious and stressed, so I was open to anything that might help me feel better. Well, I quickly got over my hesitation, because yoga immediately calmed me down. After just one hour of yoga, my overactive mind came to a standstill, and the tension in my body disappeared. Just like that. It was really powerful.

There are many different kinds of yoga (hatha, Kundalini, Bikram, and restorative, for example), but the basic principle for all of them is the same. You stretch, flex, contract, and release various muscles through a series of movements and positions that require your physical strength as well as mental concentration and focus. Not only is yoga a serious workout (make no mistake: it'll physically kick your ass), but many of the positions are specifically designed to release tension and stress. Add to that, yoga wakes you up to the right here, right now because it requires you to concentrate on your breathing. When all your mental and physical energy is focused on slowly inhaling and exhaling while balancing on one leg with your arms straight up in the air, your worries, fears, stress, and tension can no longer command your attention. Yoga forces you out of your head and connects you to your inner power.

## HOLD UP

## Yogi Power

A lot of people snub yoga because they don't consider it a "real" workout. They see a bunch of yogis stretched out on pink and purple mats in a dimly lit room and think, *I could burn out my muscles much betta' by lifting weights (and not look like a fool).* As someone who does both, I can confidently say that this assumption isn't true.

Many of the yoga postures and positions work hard-to-reach small muscles that you just can't get to with a straight weight workout. And the truth is, a sixty-second glut stretch can be much more intense than burning through ten reps of leg squats on a Smith machine. In many ways, yoga is much "tougher" than a weight workout.

Don't believe me? Afraid you'll look like a poser? Rent a couple of yoga videos from Netflix and try them in the privacy of your own home. I bet you change your mind, and when you do, I'll be waiting for you in class.

---

Today, I recommend yoga to all the gorillas at my gym. I converted a buddy of mine whom you'd never expect to see in the lotus position. He's humongous, a real monster, and watching him do yoga is pretty hilarious, but he doesn't care what he looks like. He regularly shows up in his wifebeater and Under Armour shorts because he now understands the physical and mental benefits of doing so. To the other guys who hate on yoga and look at me sideways when I suggest they give it a try, I say, "Get over yourself. You've got to trust me on this. Just one class could help you in ways you wouldn't imagine." For example, if you're feeling nervous about an upcoming job interview or a meeting with your boss, one hour of yoga might be all you need to clear your mind and boost your confidence. Yoga forces you to relax, and the truth is that your body can't be relaxed and anxious at the same time.

And if that's not enough, as a side benefit for you juice bags, yoga class is a great place to meet girls. I'm sure it depends on where you live, but on Staten Island, I'm usually one of only two guys in a class full of super hot girls in sexy yoga pants. For the record, I don't creep on girls in yoga class, but the odds are in my favor; the opportunity is certainly there.

## Cool Down, Calm Down

Working out is one of the most effective, actionable, and natural ways I know of to shut down the negativity of my mind and connect me to my inner power. If I start my workout at a low energy level, 99 percent of the time I leave feeling physically and mentally invigorated. Plus there's a real sense of satisfaction to be gained for being proactive and doing something healthy to redirect your negative energy in a positive way.

I'd hope that this endorsement alone would be enough to motivate you to get up off the couch and down to your local gym *stat*, but understanding why you should work out and actually doing it are two different things entirely. The mental workout below is designed to give you the motivation you need to take that first step.

### VINNY'S MENTAL WORKOUT

## Do Whatever You Can, Whenever You Can

I'm not a dietician, a weight loss expert, a professional coach, or a trainer, but I do have some general advice: do whatever you can, whenever you can. While research indicates that at least thirty minutes of moderate-intensity exercise three to five days a week will produce the most beneficial results, I can confidently tell you that any amount of physical exercise will generally help lift you up and improve your mood. As an added bonus, exercise often boosts your self-esteem and confidence too.

My advice? Start by figuring out what physical activity you most enjoy doing, and do it as frequently as you can. And—*this is key*—when you're doing it, give it all you've got.

It really doesn't matter what you do. Seriously, you could jump in place for an hour, or practice the Jersey Turnpike in front of your bathroom mirror until sweat pours down your back. As long as it gets your blood pumping and is an activity that pushes you to work hard, you're on the right track.

As I mentioned earlier, I do a combination of cardio, weight training, and yoga classes three to five days a week. I realize this might sound ambitious, and maybe even unrealistic to you. Take into consideration that it took me a while to work up to this routine, and to be honest, it doesn't always happen, but that's the goal I've set for myself. I've discovered that when I get that much physical exercise, I feel my best. I'm at the top of my mental game, so to speak.

You will want to create a routine that works based on what makes you feel the best. This isn't a competition; it's about designing the best workout for you, so try not to fall into the trap of comparing yourself with other people (remember: that's just your insecure ego talking smack). What activities make *you* feel the best physically and mentally? Do you know what they are? Spend some time figuring it out.

Once you have your answer, set a reasonable goal for yourself and then stick to it. I've read research that says that significantly reducing stress through exercise doesn't happen overnight. You must exercise consistently for at least several weeks to really notice a decrease in mental tension, so the key is to keep at it. Work hard. Do what you can, when you can, and you will begin to notice that how good you feel mentally is directly related to how good you feel physically. As Wayne Dyer says, "Every activity has an energy field," so participate in high-energy activities as much as possible. Exercise is one of them.

## Sleep: The Horizontal Workout

Not only does exercise do a great job at redirecting negative thoughts and releasing bottled-up physical stress, it also improves your overall health, including your ability to get a good night's sleep.

Sleep is so important; I cannot stress this enough. How much you're getting or not getting can make or break you. Now I admit I'm like a lot of young people who tend to stay up late, and sometimes all night. When I'm shooting *Jersey Shore,* my roommates and I will stay out until the clubs close, party after hours at the house, and often stay up until three and four in the morning. If I'm not careful, this can do a real number on both my body and my mind. The truth is, if you don't get enough sleep (six to eight hours is what most doctors recommend), you set yourself up for mental warfare. You may begin to notice that your thoughts begin to run wild and that your energy shifts into low gear, along with your mood. More seriously, lack of sleep can lead to acute anxiety and depression. I've certainly experienced both firsthand.

During season 5 of *Jersey Shore,* I had a series of sleepless nights that kicked off the return of my anxiety in a major way. It was my own fault; I should have seen it coming. We'd just returned from Italy, where we'd partied like it was spring break for six solid weeks. Then we jumped back into our old lifestyle in the States, which was just as insane. I was partying hard nearly every night and then trying to make up for it by napping during the day. This strategy didn't work. I was running on fumes. I spent most of my waking hours feeling sluggish, irrational, and irritable, and eventually, despite my extreme fatigue, I developed insomnia (and that annoying eye twitch). All I wanted to do was sleep, but my mind wouldn't let me. It was torture! It finally came to a point where I was so physically exhausted and mentally drained that I pleaded with the producers of the show to put me up in a hotel room for a night—just so I could catch up on some much needed rest.

Everyone on the show recognized that I was really struggling, so the producers agreed to give me a break. This scene never made it onto any of the final shows, but my producers set me up in a nearby hotel for one night, and while a solid six-hour block of sleep definitely helped to recharge me, it wasn't enough to totally revive me. I'd run myself down to the point of depletion. I felt like I had nothing left to give. I returned to the Seaside house knowing that I would need a more aggressive plan of attack to beat my anxiety before it totally beat me down.

## HOLD UP

## Sleepless Nights

Does it matter when you go to sleep as long as you're getting enough sleep? I've asked various doctors about this because, like a lot of young people, I've often tried to catch up on my sleep in the middle of the day, only to wake up hours later feeling just as tired, or like I have a nasty hangover (whether I drank the night before or not).

It turns out that the body gets its best rest at night, when the lights are out and it's dark outside. Under these conditions, the body releases melatonin, also known as the "hormone of darkness" and the "Dracula of hormones." Melatonin is triggered by darkness; it's released into your bloodstream around nine every night and makes you feel drowsy so that you fall asleep. It hangs around in your body until about nine the next morning, after the sun comes up. Notice I said it's triggered by darkness, so brave the bogeyman and turn off the lights!

When you sleep during the day (or with the lights on at night), you basically screw with the release of melatonin, and this throws off your body's natural rhythms. This means that you wake up feeling just as tired as you were when you closed your eyes, and if you make a prolonged habit of shifting your sleep to daytime hours, you may gain weight and develop more serious issues like insomnia, acute anxiety, and depression.

I understand that it's not always easy to go to bed at a reasonable hour, but without enough sleep, your physical and mental state will more than likely suffer. Make a habit of checking in with how you feel. If you're not feeling good, consider making nighttime sleep a priority. You can always hit the late-night clubs *next* weekend.

---

# Recharge

Like me, you're human. From time to time, you're going to skimp on sleep, overdo it on junk food, slack off at the gym, and potentially fall into a mental slump. Don't freak. Should you find yourself in any one of these situations, instead of further beating yourself up, just pick yourself back up off the floor and get back in the game. Dragging yourself out of bed and to the gym when you're feeling shitty can seem like an impossible task, but getting physical exercise is one of the most accessible tools you can use that will quickly help you to feel better. Remember, do whatever you can, whenever you can. Get outside and take a short walk around the block. Do a half-ass workout. Just get moving. You'll feel better as soon as you do. Guaranteed.

# IN THE REAL WORLD: Check Yourself Before You Wreck Yourself

I'll be the first one to encourage you to have your fun. Party until the sun comes up if you want to; just be sure to get back on the program before you become vulnerable to physical and mental stress. I've overdone it enough times by now to know what I am and what I'm not capable of. Do you know *your* limits?

When I'm traveling to do club appearances, guest star on a TV show, or attend an awards show, for example, my schedule will often look like this: take a cross-country flight; cab it to my hotel; quickly nap, shower, and dress; and go directly to my event. Afterward, I'll meet up with business associates, have some drinks, grab a late-night dinner, hit the after-hours clubs with friends, cab it back to the hotel, sleep for two hours, and then head straight for the airport.

This is a fun schedule to keep, but to be honest, I can only do about one twenty-four-hour cycle of this craziness without its destroying me. As soon as I land back in New York and get home to Staten Island, I must immediately catch up on my sleep and get back to the gym before my high-class lifestyle (I'm not complaining) takes its toll.

My advice? Check yourself before you wreck yourself. Know your limits, and do what you can to stay within those boundaries. If you push yourself too far, rein yourself back in as soon as you can. By all means, have your fun, but then—get back to it! Jump back into the program as soon as tomorrow.

# Moving On . . .

Not only will high-energy physical exercise help you quiet your mind and connect you to your inner power, it will release the physical signs of your stress. You'll likely notice that general aches and pains associated with tension, anxiety, and stress ease up once you start regularly moving that body of yours. And as if that weren't enough, exercise will get you into shape. You'll look better and feel more confident. Ironically, when I'm at my lowest mentally, I physically look my best because I'm hitting the gym sometimes five to seven days a week in an effort to work out my high anxiety. That said, I don't recommend stress as a reliable weight loss plan. If you want to drop a few pounds, my best advice is to change how you eat. In the next chapter, "Keep It Clean," I'll explain how when you combine clean eating with physical exercise, you put yourself in an even stronger position to control the crazy.

# 5
# KEEP IT CLEAN

**N**ow look, I'm the first to admit that I splurge on unhealthy foods from time to time. After-hours post-club food on the Shore includes chicken fingers, cheese balls, french fries, and corn dogs—anything and everything greasy and fried. Like I've said, I'm not perfect. I'm human. But in general, I make a habit of eating foods that I know will make me feel good physically and mentally. I call this making the choice between eating low- versus high-energy foods.

In this chapter, "Keep It Clean," I'll tell you what I know about:

- The effects of sugar, salt, and caffeine on your mood

- Choosing high-energy, "stress-free" foods

- Vitamins and natural feel-good remedies

- How to bounce back from a splurge

- My philosophy on drugs and alcohol

## Low- versus High-Energy Foods

For many of us, low-energy foods are some of the most fun to eat because not only do they taste good, we tend to put them on the "forbidden" shelf. What we can't have, we want, right? I'm talking about sugary stuff like cupcakes, cookies, and candy; processed, boxed foods that are high in salt, preservatives, and artificial flavorings; heavy carbs like white bread, potatoes, and pasta; and foods high in saturated fat, like a greasy hamburger and fries. I know many of these foods are tempting and taste mad good, but the downside is that they often leave you feeling tired, sluggish, and mentally shot. Remember, your mind and physical body are connected, so what you put into your body has a direct effect on your mood. If your mind feels like a greasy cheeseburger, chances are—you just ate one!

Considering this, every time you eat, you have an important choice to make. Will you choose foods that leave you feeling good, both physically and mentally, or not? It seems like a no-brainer decision to make, except for the simple fact that most of us eat foods based on how great they look and taste, and totally disregard how they'll make us feel afterward. Many experts in the field of spirituality and personal growth believe that in order to align yourself with positive "high energy," you must eat high-energy foods. Said another way: if you want to connect to your inner power—the cool, calm force inside you that doesn't act and react like a fool—you must remove foods and substances from your diet that jam up the connection.

I'm not a dietician or a nutritionist. I have no magic food plan for you to follow, just general advice: steer clear of foods that make you feel physically spent (that is, heavy, lethargic, and weak) and also knock you down emotionally. Period.

This is not complicated. It's simple. Yet everyone's body is a little bit different, which means that it's *your* responsibility to become mindful of how different foods individually affect you, and how much of them you can get away with eating. Think of it this way—personal responsibility is your new food plan.

To make it even simpler, I'll break it down for you. Following are some low-energy foods you should watch out for, as they are sure to bring down your mood.

## Jumping Permitted

If you're someone who doesn't feel the need to be schooled on hitting the gym and eating right (you've already got a bangin' hot body and a diet that's working wonders for you), then you have my permission to jump forward to the next chapter, "You Gotta Breathe." All my mental, physical, and spiritual tricks support and build on one another, but they're also effective on their own. So, even though I'm pretty convinced that this chapter has something to offer everyone (yes—*even you,* the hottest girl ever), feel free to jump around within my mind-body-spirit "triple-threat" program. Just remember, the benefit of getting your physical body in shape is that in addition to looking and feeling good, your mind and spirit also get a major workout. Bottom line: how you treat your body directly impacts how you think and how you feel. To be sure you understand just how your morning coffee and the late afternoon candy bar are affecting your mind, body, *and* spirit, you may want to stay right where you are and keep reading.

---

## Sugar

From time to time, I make a special dessert called Vinny's Chocolate Cookie Concoction for my *Jersey Shore* roommates. I throw together the ingredients contained in one box of Betty Crocker Ultimate Chocolate Chip Cookies mix, but instead of making individual cookies, I spread all the batter out in one pan and bake one gigantic cookie. After it comes out of the oven and has a chance to cool, I cover it with vanilla ice cream and mounds of chocolate sauce and whipped cream. We all crowd around the pan and dig in. We don't stop eating until it's gone. Then, we all want to die. (Ronnie usually stinks up the bathroom the entire night after one of these bad boys.)

Eating dessert can be a hell of a lot of fun, but just beware: sweets can really screw with your blood sugar levels. When you eat something like brownies, chocolate cream pie, or my favorite, tiramisu, your blood sugar level shoots straight off the chart, releasing insulin, the hormone in our bodies designed to regulate and bring our blood sugar level back down to a safe range. Except if we eat too much sugar too quickly, our body goes into high-alert mode; it releases a powerhouse amount of insulin that causes our blood sugar to drop crazy fast, creating the sugar "crash" most of us are familiar with. A crash may mean you suddenly feel tired and run-down, irritable, and moody. It can also shift an overanxious mind back into high gear.

For these reasons, I generally stay away from desserts and foods with hidden sugars. A Devil Dog is legitimately tasty, but given the choice, I'd rather feel calm and clear and free of amped-up crazy thoughts. Trust me, Devil Dog "crazy" happens to me. Just one of these chocolaty, cakey desserts can spin me into a "my life sucks" low-down mood that lasts all afternoon. Plus I don't have to tell you that sweets aren't good for your physical body. Everyone knows that a lot of sugar in your diet will expand your waistline (which means you can't rock your skinny jeans). I'm not an expert on nutrition, but I've learned to follow a very straightforward plan that sounds ridiculously obvious, and yet works: experiment with different foods and see how you feel. If sugar brings you down, don't eat it.

## Caffeine

If you, like me, have an overactive anxious mind, or just a mind that takes a run on you from time to time, you may also consider dialing your caffeine intake way back. I'm Italian. Naturally, I love espresso. But unfortunately, caffeine tends to jack me up and spin my mind out of control. If I'm already feeling nervous, jumpy, or stressed in any way, I must pass on it. Or I'm screwed.

In Italy, when I was filming season 4 of *Jersey Shore,* I got extremely drunk one night and stayed up until seven thirty in the morning. I had to show up to work at the O'Vesuvio pizzeria at ten. (Very stupid. Not a good example of planning ahead, kids.) I rolled out of bed at nine and stumbled around the house, still drunk from the night before. It was, or rather *I* was—a total joke.

I made it to the pizzeria on time, but I was in no condition to work. I was sluggish and weak. My boss, Marco, took one look at me and proceeded to make me a steaming cup of espresso. I downed it, and within minutes my body started to retaliate. I was standing by the hot ovens when I started pouring sweat. I looked down at my hands, and they were shaking. My heart started going a mile a minute, and I had the sudden urge to run to the bathroom. *Shit!* I was all too familiar with this feeling of being overly caffeinated, and I knew there was really no way to get rid of it other than to ride it out.

One shot of espresso won't typically screw with me this much, but because I'd already been in a low place to start with that morning, the caffeine just made matters worse. My emotional symptoms soon caught up with my physical reaction. I couldn't concentrate; I became dizzy and overly anxious. I told Marco, "I'm not feeling so good." Eventually, he sent me outside with a sandwich, where I sat on the sidewalk with a sign that read, "Help me, I'm hungover."

It's a known fact: caffeine in coffee, soft drinks, some teas, and popular energy drinks like Red Bull and Rockstar can seriously aggravate an already anxious mind. As it is with sugar, caffeine tends to give you a quick jolt of energy followed by a crash that can leave you feeling lethargic and low. Plus, when you drink it late in the day, it can screw with your sleep patterns.

It's funny to think about now, but my experience at O'Vesuvio that morning just goes to show how powerful the adverse effects of caffeine can be on your physical and mental state, especially when you're already feeling vulnerable.

Experiment and learn what your limits are. Your caffeine tolerance might be very different from mine. (Even when I *am* feeling relatively chill, the smallest hit of caffeine has the potential to kick my anxious mind into gear.) If you can drink it without so much as a heart flutter, go ahead—enjoy an extra-frothy cappuccino on me. If, on the other hand, you *do* discover that caffeine heightens your level of stress, dial it back. While this can be difficult at first—especially if you're in the habit of grabbing a Starbucks or a Coffee Bean every morning or chugging an energy drink before heading out for the night—you will likely discover that once caffeine is out of your system, you'll feel more clear and calm. In fact, don't be surprised if you feel more alert and awake!

## Salt

Most processed foods, like crackers, chips, and most anything that comes in a bag or a box, are heavily coated in salt. Sure, salt makes food extra tasty, but it also increases your blood pressure and depletes your body of potassium, which is essential for a properly functioning nervous system. In short, salt can mess with your brain, making you vulnerable to added stress. For this reason, you may consider cutting it out of your diet, or at least decreasing how much of it you consume.

> VINNY'S MENTAL WORKOUT

## Check Yourself

My advice is simple: figure out what foods work best for you by becoming mindful of how they make you feel physically and mentally. How do you do this? Check in with your body before you eat, just after you eat, and several times throughout the day.

For example, do you go into a meal feeling famished and run-down? If so, you may not be eating the right amount of foods that give you long-term, sustainable energy. After finishing a meal, do you feel alert and energized or heavy and lethargic? If you feel heavy, your portion size may be too big, or maybe you're eating foods with hidden sugars that give you a quick lift before dropping you three stories. Also ask yourself, How do I feel throughout the day? Cool, calm, and alert or crazy and stressed? If it's the latter, maybe there's too much salt and caffeine in your diet.

Become super aware of how you feel physically and mentally. If you're feeling bad, take a good look at what you're putting in your body. And then don't be surprised at what you discover. A double order of chili cheese fries at midnight is probably not going to sit well with you the next day. A cupcake and a double espresso for lunch probably won't give you the right amount of energy to carry you throughout the afternoon. Be aware of, and take personal responsibility for, how your food choices affect you physically and mentally. Only you control what goes into your body, so it's up to you to decide what's best for you.

Bottom line: create physical and mental balance in your life by checking in with your body. What foods make you feel the best? What foods make you feel weak? How much food is too much food? To maintain a clear, calm mind, it's extremely important that you know the answers to these questions. If you don't, it's time to *check yourself.*

## Stress-Free Foods

So now that you know what foods are likely to mess with your emotional state, what are the foods that will make it easier for you to maintain a cool, calm state of mind? I call foods that make me feel good "high-energy, stress-free foods," and they consist primarily of lean proteins, whole grains, and fresh fruits and vegetables. I've discovered that when I leave the processed foods on the shelf and eat a diet of simple and natural foods, my mental and physical energy stand a much stronger chance of remaining upbeat.

## Lean Protein

Lean proteins such as chicken, turkey, and seafood are great because they digest slowly in your stomach, making you feel fuller longer and provide you with long-term energy. I've discovered that it's fairly easy to eat this way if you're dining out, but if I'm home, it's more of a challenge. My mom is famous for her fried chicken cutlets, beef meatballs, and sausage pizza. It's so tempting to eat whatever's she's cooking—and a lot of it. And while many of her Sicilian dishes digest slowly and give me an energy reserve, they're often high in carbs and fat. If I'm not careful, I'll get up from the table feeling physically heavy, and this can put a drain on my mental energy. *Sorry, Ma! Your food's delicious, but sometimes I just have to resist it!*

## Whole Grains

There's a big difference between simple carbs and complex carbs. Simple carbs like bread and pasta made with white flour and most packaged cereals generally give you a quick spike in energy followed by a crash that can trigger feelings of fatigue and a low mood. Complex carbs, on the other hand, like whole-grain breads and pasta, oats, brown rice, nuts, and beans, are absorbed into the body more slowly and stay in your system for a while, giving you long-term physical and mental energy. For an even better energy boost, combine lean proteins with whole grains, like grilled chicken with brown rice. The protein will slow the digestion process down even more, giving you an added reserve of positive energy.

## Fruits and Vegetables

Eat your fruits and veggies. Not only will this make your mother proud, your body and mind will thank you for it too. Fresh produce is packed with nutrients and natural fiber that digests slowly, helping you maintain consistent physical and mental energy.

When it comes to fruit juice, take it easy. Naked's Green Machine Super Food is my favorite afternoon pick-me-up, but because juice is basically fruit that's been stripped of most of its fiber, its natural sugars tend to rush into the bloodstream quickly, spiking my energy and then dropping me fast. For this reason, I have to be careful how much, and how quickly, I drink it. The best solution I've found is to eat something along with my favorite juice smoothies, like a handful of nuts or a granola bar, to slow down the digestion process and avoid a sugar crash. If you notice that the natural sugars from fruit or fruit juice leave you feeling ultimately sluggish, then cut back on how much of it you eat and drink. Remember, it's all on you.

## Water

Staying hydrated is very important. Water carries essential hormones and nutrients to vital organs in your body. If your body isn't well hydrated, you run the risk of experiencing unpleasant physical and mental side effects, including an increase in anxiety, nervousness, disorientation, and fatigue. Interesting fact: I've read that lack of water is the number one trigger of daytime fatigue. I'm a water freak; I try to drink at least ten glasses a day. The recommended amount is eight glasses daily, but simply increasing from the amount you drink now is a positive first step. I've discovered that if I'm feeling run-down, a tall, cold glass of water is sometimes all it takes to give me the mental boost I need to snap me awake mentally and physically.

# My Diet

On a good day, I eat eggs, whole wheat toast, and some fresh fruit for breakfast. For lunch, I have a high-powered protein shake with chocolate whey protein and a banana. For dinner, I typically eat a lean protein like grilled chicken breast, grass-fed beef, or salmon with a huge helping of organic veggies on the side. If I'm still hungry after all that, I'll eat a piece of fruit for dessert.

This might not sound like much food, but for me it's just the right amount, and more important, it keeps me in a calm, clear, and positive state of mind. Plus I find that when I eat natural and simple foods that boost me mentally, I have more energy to focus on creative and intellectual pursuits like acting, writing, drawing, reading, and furthering my education. And as an additional bonus, when I eat this way, I lose any extra meat I might have collected around my belly. When I start to complicate my diet with foods that aren't natural and fresh, I run the risk of gaining weight and becoming mentally distracted. Bottom line: it's my fear of becoming physically and mentally wrecked that helps me avoid the second helpings and the low-energy junk food. For me, eating crap is just not worth the risk.

### HOLD UP

## Loss of Appetite?

Loss of appetite is fairly typical for people who struggle with anxiety, tension, and general stress. What I've learned is that when your body is in high-stress mode, it sends blood away from the stomach and the digestive system and into the muscles in your arms and legs so that you can either physically fight or run away from whatever's threatening you. When you're in this "fight or flight" survival mode, it's common to lose your sense of appetite, even though you may be physically hungry.

During season 5 of *Jersey Shore,* I completely lost my appetite and eventually stopped eating. As you can imagine, I lost a considerable amount of weight. People were stopping me on the street and saying things like "What's wrong, bro? No more gym?" I knew I needed to eat a diet rich in high-energy, stress-free foods to regain my mental and physical strength, but it wasn't until after losing nearly twenty pounds and hardly recognizing the skinny kid in the bathroom mirror that I jumped back into my program. And let me tell you—it wasn't easy. I had to force myself to start eating healthy again and regularly returning to the gym.

You may be reading this and thinking, *I'd love to lose twenty pounds! Sign me up for Vinny's stress diet!* If so, let me stop you right there. Dropping weight because you're physically and mentally wrecked is not the way to go. It's dangerous. If life has knocked you down in any way—you've lost your job, ended a relationship, bombed a test, or had a falling-out with a family member—abandoning a healthy diet in stressful times will further weaken you. And if you're not careful, you can weaken yourself to a point where it feels impossible to regain your strength. This is what happened to me.

It's so important that you keep your body well fed. Don't forget, the connection between your physical and mental body is crazy important.

## Vitamins and Natural "Feel Good" Remedies

In addition to eating high-energy, stress-free foods, I also include a variety of vitamins and natural supplements in my diet, like wheatgrass, for the extra mental lift. (*Warning: wheatgrass burps taste like your front lawn.*)

I've learned that not only will certain vitamins give you a mental boost, but also a deficiency of them can contribute to feelings of stress, tension, and anxiety. Not to worry. Vitamins and supplements aren't hard to find. They used to be available only in hippie health food stores, but now they're shelved at your corner Duane Reade, Walgreens, or CVS, which means they're easy to integrate into your diet.

## HOLD UP

## No Magic Pill

I may have figured out a few things about treating my body right, but I'm not a nutritionist. If you think you have a vitamin deficiency, consult with your doctor or a health care professional before taking any nutritional supplements. A health care professional can also help you determine the appropriate dosage for you. Also, vitamin supplements by themselves are not enough to manage high stress and anxiety levels. Taking supplements is just a tool that when combined with others in your toolbox will help you combat general negativity and a low mood. Vitamins alone will not fix anything.

The vitamin at the top of my list is B12. I refer to it as my "personal savior." When I was at my lowest point during season 5 of *Jersey Shore,* I visited a doctor and unloaded my history. I explained to him how my anxiety had turned chronic, how tired I felt, that I had bad headaches, and that I couldn't sleep because of an annoying cough that wouldn't go away. Just as I've been explaining to you, he stressed the importance of physical self-care as a way to counteract my mental vulnerabilities. To jump-start my recovery, he gave me a shot of vitamin B12.

## Vitamin B

Vitamins B6 and B12 are important for the maintenance of a healthy nervous system (that is, your mental health). Being on edge over a long period of time can create a deficiency of this vitamin in your body, which can in turn create *more* anxiety and, in some cases, concentration problems, loss of appetite, and insomnia, so do yourself a favor, and make sure you're getting enough of it. As an alternative to taking a vitamin B supplement, you can boost your vitamin B levels by eating lean red meats, fish, clams, poultry, some fortified cereals, and dairy products such as yogurt, milk, and cheese. When I regularly take a vitamin B supplement, I feel a noticeable lift of fatigue and irritability.

### HOLD UP

## Chemical X

Cortisol is called the "stress hormone" because it's secreted into the bloodstream in times of heightened stress. (In season 5 of *Jersey Shore,* my doctor and I referred to it as "Chemical X.") Its positive effects include a quick burst of energy, increased immunity, and a lower sensitivity to pain. However, when the body undergoes prolonged tension and stress, larger doses of cortisol are released into the blood for longer periods of time, and this can have *negative* effects, including a rattled mind and a spike in blood pressure. This is what happened with me. My chronic anxiety jacked up my cortisol level to a point where my body was unable to regulate it.

To keep your cortisol level healthy and under control, it's important to put stress management strategies into place, like getting regular physical exercise and maintaining a diet rich in high-energy, stress-free foods and natural supplements to relax your body and mind.

---

## Vitamin C

I've read studies that link the stabilization of cortisol, the "stress hormone," in the body to vitamin C. This may be why many experts suggest that people with plenty of vitamin C in their diets recover faster from stress than those with low levels. Vitamin C has also been linked to boosting immunity and protecting the body against sickness and infection in times of heightened tension. As an alternative to taking a vitamin C supplement, add oranges, pineapples, papayas, kiwi, blueberries, cranberries, tomatoes, spinach, broccoli, avocados, and red bell peppers to your diet. If you can't get your hands on fresh produce, try taking Emergen-C. You've probably seen this dietary supplement at your local corner market or grocery store (if not, ask for it. Almost everyone carries it now). Emergen-C comes in many flavors and packs 1,000 milligrams of vitamin C into each packet. Mix it with water and drink.

## Calcium and Magnesium

Calcium keeps our teeth and bones healthy and strong and also maintains the functioning of our heart and nerves. The reason you often see calcium and magnesium bottled together in the supplements aisle is because magnesium helps regulate our calcium levels. The two go hand in hand.

When we're tense and under stress, our bodies can become depleted of magnesium, which in turn messes with our body's ability to absorb calcium. Not good. A depletion of magnesium can also have negative mental consequences, including agitation and a heightened sense of anxiety; in some cases, a depletion can trigger insomnia and depression. As an alternative to taking a magnesium supplement, try increasing your consumption of nuts, beans, green leafy vegetables, tofu, and chocolate.

## Omega-3 Oils

Although the findings are mixed, many experts believe that omega-3 oils are good for our mental health, including treating and preventing chronic anxiety and depression, as well as generally boosting our brainpower, memory, and mood. Unfortunately, our bodies don't naturally produce omega-3 oils, so in order to increase our supply, we have to either take a supplement or eat foods that are rich in them. Flaxseed, salmon, sardines, broccoli, and walnuts are great ways to get your daily fix.

## Essential Oils

In addition to taking natural supplements, I've also discovered the benefit of essential oils to reduce tension, mental exhaustion, anxiety, agitation, and basic burnout. Don't laugh, but I buy lavender oil as a spray and mist my room whenever I'm having an overly anxious moment. I said, *Don't laugh!* For real, it helps with relaxation. I also shower with chamomile soap to help calm my nerves and bring myself back into mental balance, and I use tea tree oil in the form of soap, shampoo, and pure oil that I rub on my wrists to reinvigorate and wake me up. My sister is the vegan-yogi type and turned me on to all of this stuff. You can find essential oils and all kinds of aromatic self-care products at your local health food store. Whole Foods has a pretty dope selection. The idea of my lathering up with

a bar of soap that has "healing properties" may sound like a joke to
you. Go ahead and make fun of me, but I'm telling you—don't hate
on natural remedies. These simple tools work!

## How to Bounce Back from a Splurge

Do I always eat the right foods, take my vitamins, and drink enough
water? Of course not. If you watch me on *Jersey Shore,* you've seen
me stuff my face at Sunday dinner countless times. I'm not perfect.
And I'm Italian! Food—and lots of it—has always been a big part
of my life.

Instead of striving for perfection, I focus on balance. As a general
rule, I can safely allow myself one to two "cheat" days a week when I
indulge in lower-energy foods, but I have to check in with my mood
first to determine how far I can go. If I'm already feeling anxious or
low, I know a trip to Rivoli's on the Shore is a very bad idea. Their
chicken parmesan on top of a pound of pasta once put me in a food
coma that lasted for hours. In addition to feeling like a gluttonous
pig, I was mentally wrecked. My advice: check in with your state of
mind before you stuff your face.

If you *do* eat something that throws you out of whack mentally,
make a note of what it is, and then engage in an activity to bring
yourself back into balance. Remember, a setback can quickly be cor-
rected by spending an hour at the gym and by making your next
meal one that is fresh, clean, and simple. When you stick to a clean,
stress-free food plan as a general rule, you can occasionally dabble
in low-energy foods (like after you've stumbled home drunk from a
club) without the negative mental and physical consequences being
so harsh.

> **VINNY'S MENTAL WORKOUT**
>
> ## Choose to Feel Good
>
> Before indulging in low-energy foods or abusive substances, check yourself on the Negativity-o-Meter, where 5 is "I'm in a dark place" and 1 is "I'm feeling pretty peaceful and chill." If you're already at a 5, you may want to forgo the greasy pizza and pitcher of beer. Chances are good that this combo will leave you feeling physically gross, and mentally shot as well. Remember, what you put into your body is your choice. If you make choices that leave you feeling bad, you have no one else to blame but yourself. My advice? Choose to feel good. If you do eat foods that set you back (no worries—it happens!), use the tools you've learned in this chapter to start feeling good again.

# Thoughts on Drugs and Alcohol

What about drugs and alcohol, you ask? Let me first say: no judgment. *I'll do me, and you do you.* That said, I'm personally not into doing drugs, simply because they can quickly spin me out of control, mentally and physically, and this frightens me. Having control over my mind is how I feel a sense of personal power, so I just say no. (Maybe you've seen me on *Jersey Shore* wearing a T-shirt advocating "Pugs, Not Drugs.") All jokes aside, it's not my place to preach. What *you* do is your call entirely. But consider asking yourself, *How do drugs make me feel?* If your answer is, *Not so good,* you might consider changing your behaviors so you *do* feel good.

When it comes to drinking, I don't have to tell you what side of the party line I'm on. Millions of viewers have seen me doing shots of Patrón on national TV. And it's not because some producer is forcing them down my throat. Every time I drink, I alone make the conscious decision to do so. For whatever reason, the physical and mental affects of alcohol are much easier for me to manage and control than recreational drugs, so I will indulge. Still, I have to be careful. Just like with foods, I always assess where my mind is *before* I start lining up shots. Most of the time, I can handle my drink. I'm one of those "happy drunks." I get silly on the dance floor, crack a lot of jokes, and often pass out grinning from ear to ear. That said, I've been in dark mental slumps where drinking alcohol has only made matters worse. The fact is—alcohol is a depressant, and I've learned the hard way that if I'm already feeling anxious, stressed, or low-down, alcohol will only serve to bring me down even lower. Not only that, but a nasty hangover can set me back mentally for days. Knowing this, in troubled times I'm smart to slow my drinking way down—or stay away from it altogether. During season 4 of *Jersey Shore,* I drank every day and seriously paid for it. These days, I try to take it easy. If I'm going out, I try to have just two drinks per night. How do I make two drinks last throughout the night? If you've ever seen me out partying, you may notice that I'm that guy who drinks glasses of water in between drinks. This slows me down and keeps me hydrated.

As for you, I'm not going to tell you how much to drink. Again, you have to make that call for yourself. What I will recommend is that you become conscious of how alcohol affects you. Know what it does to you mentally and physically, and make smart decisions based on your own personal insight. Also, and I know it's not always easy, but I urge you to resist any social pressure that tells you to drink beyond your limits. Have fun, but also take care of yourself. If you know that two drinks is all you can handle (three turns you into a belligerent hot mess), do yourself a favor and stop after two! And if the people you're partying with don't respect your personal drink limit, consider whether their pushy, drunk-ass energy is the kind you want to be around.

## IN THE REAL WORLD: Drink Responsibly

Drinking alcohol can be a lot of fun. I'd be a hypocrite if I told you to stop drinking and hang up your party hat. In my opinion, there's nothing wrong with indulging in a cocktail, or a *few*, if you're of age. Just be aware of what it will do to you. For some people, alcohol has no negative effects. For others, it leaves them physically and mentally depleted. If you've ever had a serious hangover, you're probably familiar with the feeling of dehydration that goes along with drinking too much. Remember, dehydration can lead to an increase in anxiety, nervousness, stress, and fatigue. Plus alcohol can screw with your sleep patterns, which can also negatively impact your mood. And to top it all off, alcohol can compromise your sense of judgment and accountability, getting you in all sorts of trouble. If you've ever woken up with a missing tooth or a penis drawn on the side of your face, you know what I'm talking about.

Now hear me out: I'm not trying to be a buzzkill. Go ahead—go a little WILD. Just become aware of what your body and mind can handle and plan accordingly. The decision is always yours. Remember, the goal isn't perfection; it's to strive for a healthy balance.

# Moving On . . .

Getting high-energy physical exercise and eating clean don't require super human strength. You can do it. But I'm not gonna lie—it requires effort and some amount of work. Not a big deal. I've found that by simply asking myself, *Vin, do you want to feel good or bad?*, eating right and going to the gym suddenly don't feel like work. Instead, they're just choices I make that improve my quality of life.

Okay. Now that we've gotten body and diet balance out of the way, I want to introduce you to a few more tools for combating negativity that may surprise you. In the next chapter, "You Gotta Breathe," I show you how to practice one of the simplest and most powerful techniques I know of for connecting to your inner power and controlling the crazy. And you don't even have to get up from where you are now to start practicing it.

# 6
# YOU GOTTA BREATHE

**N**ow that you're committed to getting regular exercise and eating clean, let's pause for a little breather. Next, I want to introduce you to the simple act of inhaling and exhaling. In a word: breathing. It's one of the most natural things we do. Most of us don't give it any thought, and yet to *focus* on your breath is one of the most powerful and efficient physical tricks I know of to relax and quiet the mind. For this reason, it's one of my favorite go-to "emergency" tools in times of stress.

In this chapter, "You Gotta Breathe," I'll tell you what I know about:

- The connection between breathing and stress

- What meditation is: just fancy talk for deep breathing

- What yoga is: meditation mixed with movement

- What prayer is: deep breathing with words

# Blow Your Stress Away

I do a lot of club appearances that are off the wall. I walk into rooms filled with pounding music, smoke, and lights, and it's usually so packed that you can't even move. Sometimes I have thousands of fans charging me at once, trying to pour Grey Goose down my throat and asking me to sign autographs and to smile and pose for photographs. Sounds fun, right? But this is a recipe for disaster if you're having a bad day. Obviously, I don't want to suffer from an anxiety attack in the middle of signing some cute girl's *Jersey Shore* DVD or poster, so I take precautionary measures. Before I head into an environment like this, I spend a few minutes in my hotel room quietly focusing on my breath. I'll sit down in a chair or on the bed and take several long and deep breaths in and out. As soon as I do this, my heart rate slows way down. After just a few minutes, I wake up to the moment and connected to my *true self*—the Vinny who's calm and in control and not ruled by my critical, fearful ego. That's when I walk out the door and head into the madness. And guess what? Nine times out of ten, the madness doesn't touch me.

Breathing is one tool I can always pull out of my back pocket and use whenever I want. It's more accessible than going to the gym or eating right. You can do it anytime, anywhere. And it's one hundred percent effective! I often use breathing to steady my nerves when the drama-o-meter goes into the red zone on the set of *Jersey Shore.* I'll take a step back from whatever mad-crazy situation is unfolding in front of me and slowly begin to breathe. It's a super subtle move; no one knows what I'm doing, and yet it makes all the difference in the world. Well, *my* world. A few deep breaths will quiet my mind and help me maintain control in an often-uncontrollable environment.

Sound too good to be true? Or does "just breathe" sound like a stupid cliché? Are you skeptical that something as mindless as breathing can bring you down from a high-pressure moment? Well, sometimes the simplest tools are the most effective and focused; deep breathing is king at relaxing and calming the mind. And not just in extreme circumstances like being on the set of a heated reality TV show, but in most any *ordinary* situation you can think of—on the phone, at a meeting, waiting in line at the bank, looking for parking. I swear, I'm not making this up. Doctors, psychologists, and experts in the fields of personal growth and mind, body, spirit all agree—breathing is one of the best ways to lower stress in the body.

Let me explain how it works—when you maintain a steady, calm breath, your brain gets the signal from your body that everything is okay. Never mind that the world could be collapsing all around you; as long as your breathing remains calm, your mind stays calm too. Breathing, it turns out, works as an immediate calming tool on both the physical body and the brain. In situations where my anxiety begins to spin out of control, if I simply focus on, and slow down, my breathing, my mind immediately switches gears. It downshifts and slows down to match my breath. Trust me, it's a pretty cool trick.

## HOLD UP

## Pause and Take a Deep Breath

Think back to a time when you were worried, angry, or just generally stressed. What was happening with your breath? Was it rapid? Shallow? Maybe it felt like you weren't breathing at all? In times of stress, many of us hold our breath and totally forget to breathe!

Now imagine a time when you were relaxed, when life was good. What was happening with your breath? Was it deep? Steady? Calm? You may not have realized it before, but your breath mimics your mood. Knowing this, you can use it to help *dictate* your mood. In times of stress, begin to use your breath to send a signal to your mind that everything is okay. As you slow down your breath, your worrisome, anxious thoughts will slow down too.

Obviously, you know how to breathe. You wouldn't be alive if you didn't. But the kind of automatic breathing you're probably doing right now and focused, "mindful" breathing are two very different things. Remember, when you're mindful, all your attention is focused on what you're doing. Whether it be listening to music, eating breakfast, working out at the gym, or *breathing,* when you're mindful, your focus is one hundred percent on the activity you're doing in the present moment.

## VINNY'S MENTAL WORKOUT

## Keep Breathing

When my mind is going crazy and my thoughts are as wild as a Quentin Tarantino movie, I take a few minutes to focus on my breath. While thoughts aren't always easy to control, you *always* have control over your breathing, which is why I strongly encourage you to use this tool. It's free. It's quick and easy, and it's available to you at any time of the day.

The key to deep breathing is to get your entire torso into it. Take a deep breath in through your nose. Breathe in from the base of your belly until your lungs are good and full (count up to three as you do this), and then slowly blow your breath out of your mouth (your exhale should last up to five seconds). In his book *Peace Is Every Step,* Thich Nhat Hanh suggests saying the following words to yourself as you breathe in: "Breathing in, I know that I am breathing in." As you breathe out, say, "Breathing out, I know that I am breathing out." Believe it or not, stating the obvious helps you focus on your breathing even more. And the more you focus on your breath, the less you're able to focus on whatever's distracting, worrying, or freaking you out. Without even realizing it, your breath will get you out of your head and wake you up to the present moment. In case you've forgotten, when you're "present," it's as if your mind has been put on mute. And what a relief that is! Consider all the time you spend listening to the negative noise in your head. It's exhausting, isn't it? And super distracting! Breathing provides you with a mental break. Kind of like taking a power nap.

Try it right now. Lie down on your bed or on the floor, and put this book on your stomach. Breathe in and out twenty times just as I've described above, and as you do, watch the book rise and fall with the depth of your breath. Think of how dogs or babies breathe when they're napping. Their stomachs slowly go up and down, indicating that they're in a deep, peaceful sleep. If your mind starts to wander, put your hands on your stomach. Becoming aware of your body will help you regain your focus. Sometimes I imagine my breath as a color: bright yellow or pink like what you'd see in a Miami club is my standard go-to because both these colors are easy to visualize.

Once you've focused on your breath for twenty inhales and exhales, check in with how you feel. Do you feel calm? Steady? Awake? Do you feel back in control of your thoughts and emotions? Your answer should be YES! In the words of Thich Nhat Hanh, "to master our breath is to be in control of our bodies and minds."

*Be careful:* If this mental workout leaves you feeling light headed, there's a chance you're on the verge of hyperventilating. Ease up. Check in with your breathing. Make sure it's slow and comfortable, and stop right away if you start to feel dizzy.

I have a busy schedule, and I'm sure you do too, so look for moments in your day when you can concentrate on your breath and bring yourself back to the right here, right now. I mean it—breathing is just as important as remembering to put on your pants, and you can do it anywhere, so you have no excuse not to do it. Practice focused breathing while you're getting dressed, driving your car, walking the dog, waiting for the elevator, standing in line at the ATM, cleaning your room, making a sandwich, or preparing a cup of coffee. You can do it standing up, sitting down, or lying in bed. There really are no rules for breathing other than that you give it your focused, "mindful" attention.

I practice mindful breathing when my thoughts are running wild, and *also* as a preventative measure. The same way I work out to prevent feeling heavy and run-down, I breathe to prevent feeling stressed. The way I think about it is if I can avoid stress later in my day by taking a few deep breaths now, why wouldn't I?

## IN THE REAL WORLD: Take a Breather

If someone says something ugly to you that upsets you, before you react negatively (slinging vicious insults in retaliation can be so tempting), try taking ten deep breaths. By taking a breather, you just might stop an ugly situation from getting uglier. A few deep breaths might be all you need to clear your mind and respond with some level of understanding, *or* to give you the steadiness to walk away and calm down.

# Meditation: Fancy Talk for Deep Breathing

As far as I'm concerned, meditation is just fancy talk for deep breathing (as I said earlier, don't get hung up on words). I understand that many people have preconceived ideas about meditation, like you have to be some kind of yogi sitting in the middle of the woods in the lotus position to properly meditate. Not necessarily the case. When you get down to it, meditation is just the act of concentrated breathing for the purpose of quieting your mind and connecting to your true self. Remember, negativity is not your natural state of mind. You weren't born with anxiety and stress. You came into this world as a bundle of pure positive energy. By nature, *You* are calm, peaceful, happy, and secure, and believe it or not, these aren't qualities you've outgrown. You can tap in to your natural state at any time by meditating.

## BREAK IT DOWN

## Meditation

Don't be turned off by the word! Meditation is simply the act of focused, concentrated breathing as a means to quiet the mind and connect you to your inner power—a positive force that's free of anxiety, stress, judgment, and fear. This force—what I call your "inner power"—is available to you at all times because it exists in you. It is *You*. If you're feeling tense, stressed, or generally low-down, chances are good that you're disconnected from your inner power. Meditate to reconnect. And if you're already connected, meditate to *stay* connected, so that you can avoid going to those ugly, negative places.

The first time I tried meditation was when I returned home to Staten Island after the premiere season of *Jersey Shore* wrapped. I'd miraculously gotten through six intense weeks of shooting while secretly suffering from chronic anxiety. I returned home with a very clear purpose, to finally put my overactive mind in check, and I was willing to try anything. One afternoon, I ended up at a random temple for Sri Lankan monks in the ghetto. It was just me, a handful of drug addicts, a few Indian kids, and a *bunch* of monks. The temple was dark and lit only with candles and incense. We all sat on pillows in a circle as the head monk led us in a series of prayers. It was a totally peaceful scene, but to be honest—I really couldn't get into it. My overactive mind would not slow down, and add to that, my anxiety had physically manifested as restless leg syndrome. I couldn't sit still. Every two seconds, I was changing positions. I got through it, but I never went back. Instead, I used what I learned to build a practice that was more suited to me.

## VINNY'S MENTAL WORKOUT

## Take a Walk

Meditation is just fancy talk for deep breathing, so to meditate, simply focus on the rhythm of your breath. Despite what you may have been led to believe in the past, meditation is not that complicated, nor does it require a lot of time or secluding yourself in a grass hut. You can do it anytime, anywhere, and without calling attention to yourself. (That is, unless you want to. My mom has a friend who's really into the practice and isn't afraid to show it. Once she joined us for Sunday family dinner, when suddenly we realized she'd left the table to do a handstand in the corner of the room with her eyes closed. *What the hell?*)

My meditation practice is far less dramatic. I do something called a "walking meditation," which sounds exactly like what it is. I concentrate on my breathing as I walk. Sometimes I take long walks around my neighborhood in New York or in whatever city I happen to be working in. Fresh air, sun on the face, and open space put me in the perfect mood to concentrate on my breathing and snap me into the moment. Long walks work especially well when I'm trying to calm down from a highly charged situation that's made me mad or hurt me in some way. If I think I'm going to react out of fear, anger, or spite, I will remove myself from the situation, walk away, and breathe. Other times, my meditative walks are much shorter. They could last just the amount of time it takes me to get from one production room to the next, or from my parked car to wherever I'm headed for the day. Whether it's a short or a long walk, the practice is the same—focus on the simple action of inhaling and exhaling until my mind stops making noise. As soon as I do, I notice my body goes into relaxed, chill mode.

If I meditate for five to ten minutes a day, I feel good. If I spend an *hour* in walking meditation, I feel even better! My advice? Set a manageable goal for yourself, and stick to it. Consider devoting a few minutes every day to a walking meditation, and as you practice, notice how your mind clears and how much more connected you feel to your true cool, calm, and steady self.

In Wayne W. Dyer's *There's a Spiritual Solution to Every Problem,* he references an interesting study where all the people in an organized meditation group had their serotonin levels measured right before they started to meditate. (Serotonin is a neurotransmitter in the brain; the higher the amount of serotonin, the happier and calmer you are.) After several hours of meditating, the serotonin levels in nearly everyone in the group went up. Translation: Meditation improves your mood. It makes you feel good.

## Put Them in Their Place

Focused, mindful breathing relaxes your body and calms your mind, but it won't necessarily stop you from having thoughts—positive or negative. In fact, thoughts and strong emotions might actually come up as you meditate. If this happens, let it happen. In other words, don't ignore them. If a thought like *I hate my job, I need to get out of there* comes up, acknowledge the thought and then work to bring your focus back to your breath in the present moment. In a later chapter, "Always Be Grateful," I'll show you what to do with repetitive negative thoughts and feelings that just won't go away. In other words, I'll show you how to put them in their place.

## Yoga: Meditate and Move

Wanna take your meditation practice to another level? Then try yoga, which is basically deep, meditative breathing combined with physical exercise. In many ways, I credit yoga for teaching me how to breathe. It plays to my short attention span and restless need to move. Yoga combines deep breathing with physically challenging poses that keep both your body active and your mind engaged. Therefore, if you ask me, it's the perfect combination of two very important disciplines for reducing stress and anxiety in your life.

I know we already covered yoga in an earlier chapter, but I mention it here again because I want to stress how important breathing is to your yoga practice. Where I can easily get through a set of ten bicep curls without breathing (although I try not to make a habit of doing this), it's nearly impossible for me to hold a yoga pose for ten seconds without relying on my breath to get me through. I might even go so far to say that yoga *just can't happen* without focused, "mindful" breathing.

## Be a Double Threat

Stand up from wherever you are and distribute your weight equally on both feet. Focus on your breath. Count to three as you breathe in deeply and count to five as you exhale slowly. Once you've got this rhythm down, begin to shift your weight over to the left foot, lifting your right foot off the floor. Slightly bend your left knee and bring the sole of your right foot to rest on the inside of your left calf. This requires balance, so don't be surprised if you wobble around the first few times you try this. If you need to, position yourself near a wall and steady one arm on the wall for balance. Keep breathing. Press your foot into your calf and your calf into your foot to make your stance stronger. Try not to let your right hip poke out; stand as upright as you can. Continue to breathe slowly in and out. Focus your eyes on something in front of you—even if it's just a speck on the floor. This will help you keep your balance. If you're feeling extra steady, try raising your arms up toward the ceiling with your palms touching each other.

Have you got it down? Good job! You've just struck your first "tree" pose. And now let me ask you this: As you were focused on your breath and balancing on one leg, did your mind stop making noise? Did any sadness, fears, insecurities, worries, and frustration disappear? At least temporarily? I bet they did. It's nearly impossible to hold such crazy positions with a noisy mind. Yoga is a powerful tool because you're combining two disciplines—physical exercise with deep breathing—to relax your body and calm your mind. Double threat!

# Prayer: Meditation with Words

I'm a Catholic Italian. Like food, prayer has always been a big part of my life. When I was little, I was *that* kid from *A Bronx Tale*—the one who knelt by his bed every night, reciting a long list of prayers. I prayed before meals, before school exams and basketball games, and *always*—I prayed in church. Today, even though my beliefs about God have changed, I still pray. It's part of my inner framework; I can't seem to break the habit. For many people, prayer is religiously affiliated, but I no longer exclusively connect the two. In fact, I don't think you have to be "religious" at all for prayer to be meaningful. Here's why—as far as I'm concerned, prayer is just meditation, or deep, focused breathing, combined with words. The words you say could be anything—an affirmation that really speaks to you, a lyric from a favorite song, a phrase your mom or an influential teacher often said. Typically, your prayer will consist of words that hold special meaning for you. One of my personal favorites is "Let Go, Let God." I stumbled across this message while reading Wayne W. Dyer's *The Shift*. Dyer's work has been a big influence on both my life and my program, and this message of his totally resonates with me. It reminds me that I'm not in control of everything that happens around me and to let go and let God, the Universe, Life handle the rest (more on this idea of "acceptance" in chapter 8).

In times of stress or heightened anxiety, I'll close my eyes, take several deep breaths, and repeat this saying over and over again until my body relaxes and I can hear the voice of my true self saying, *Vinny, calm down. Let it go. You're fine.* When I need a little extra help, I'll pray to my grandfather Sal, who passed away and whose gold crucifix I wear every day. I'll say, "Nonno (Grandpa in Italian), I love you. Thank you for watching over me and those around me."

It's nice to have options, wouldn't you agree? So in addition to meditation and yoga, prayer is just one more tool you can use to quiet your noisy mind and connect with your inner power—a strong and steady force that's pure and free of negativity.

---

**VINNY'S MENTAL WORKOUT**

## Say It and Believe It

If your mind is taking you for a ride, try using prayer—which is simply deep, focused breathing combined with words—to regain mental control. What you say doesn't really matter so long as you use positively charged words you believe in that disrupt the flow of negative thoughts running wild in your head. My sister Antonella likes to say, "Life will always play out the way it's supposed to." Repeating positive words while focusing on your breath clears out the negative garbage in your mind and grounds you back in the present moment where *all is as it should be.*

# Moving On . . .

You now have several practical physical tools to help relax and quiet your mind and snap you out of a negative mind funk—physical exercise, stress-free eating, and focused, deep breathing. What's cool about all three of these tools is that they work powerfully on their own *and* in combination with one another. In the next chapter, "Give Until It Hurts," I'll arm you with a few less-conventional tools that have a more *spiritual* vibe for battling stress, anxiety, and your basic bad mood and that you can also immediately put to use, starting with—generosity.

# SPIRIT

# 7
# GIVE UNTIL IT HURTS

When I began my search for tools to help me with my chronic anxiety and the occasional dip into depression, I was surprised to discover how quickly and significantly *selfless service* could lift my mood. I think you'd probably agree that helping others feels good, but I'm here to tell you that the benefits go far beyond that. The act of generosity can very effectively shut down the negative noise in your head. When I'm feeling bitched around by my overactive, anxious mind, sometimes all I have to do to calm the beast and take back positive control is extend myself to another person. In this chapter, "Give Until It Hurts," I'll tell you what I know about:

- How generosity gets you out of your head

- Why lending a hand gives you "spiritual swagger"

- The secret to giving

- How what you give determines what you *get*

# Why Selfless?

A lot of kids of my generation think selfishly. And by selfish, I mean that many people are completely "me" focused. Let's be real here: *Jersey Shore* revolves around who has the biggest muscles, the best body, the most expensive shoes, and so on. On and *off* the show, I'm surrounded by people who compete over who's getting the most girls, driving the most pimp car, and popping more bottles at the club. Add to that, this kind of me-focused "selfishness" extends past material things. I hear kids and all kinds of people trying to one-up one another with their *problems*. Who's got the most debt? Relationship issues? Job dissatisfaction? One of my favorite motivational speakers, Paul Hedderman, refers to this 24/7 obsession with oneself as "self-centeredness," and he'll tell you—and I agree—it's a dead end. All this attention paid to your *self* puts your ego in the driver's seat, and you're far enough along into this program to know exactly where this leads—to feelings like frustration, sadness, jealousy, anger, fear, anxiety, and worry. And all these negative feelings have a high probability of triggering negative actions. In short, the me-centric attitude can turn the nicest person into a grade-A asshole.

I challenge the me-centric attitude held by a lot of my peers because what I've discovered is that by serving myself less and instead extending myself more to those around me, I'm a much happier, calmer, and cooler person. At least, that's what many of my fans, friends, and colleagues tell me. By making myself available to other people and giving a little extra in a variety of ways, I've gained a reputation for being a "cool, generous guy." Not only is this giving attitude working for me on the social scene, but also by making generosity a part of my daily routine, I'm better able to keep my negative mind noise and general stress level in check. Let me give you an example of how this works.

As I mentioned several chapters back, flying tends to make me anxious as hell. I feel like a sheep as soon as I get to the airport and have to deal with all the lines, security checks, and general herding of people. However, flying is unavoidable because both my lifestyle and work schedule require that I travel fairly regularly. So how do I combat the stress of getting on a plane that I worry might crash and burn with me on it? I use generosity as a tool to distract me from my fear.

To do this, as soon as I get to the airport, I become mindful of my breath (remember, slowing down your breath will slow down your worrisome mind). Once my breath is calm and steady, I start looking around for ways I can help other people and extend myself in some way. For example, I often let women traveling with kids cut in front of me in line. I might treat whoever I'm traveling with to a drink at the airline's VIP club. I joke around and make conversation with the guards in security. Once I board the plane, I help everyone who needs a hand in stashing their luggage in the overhead bins, and I make a point to smile and say hello to the flight attendants. I'll even go so far as to take pictures with all the pilots if they want. I realize this makes me sound like a do-gooder on steroids, but honestly, I'm not trying to brag to you about what a good guy I am. I practice generosity to help other people because it also helps *me*! For real, the simple act of generosity gets me out of my head, which is very important when babies crying, life rafts, and a slow, fiery death were previously the only things on my mind.

When you're selfless, you're focused on yourself *less*. Get it? So when negative thoughts run wild in your head, practice generosity to redirect your attention. Before you know it, your mind will begin to quiet down, and you'll find yourself in a much calmer, happier place. Take it from me—it works. Not only do I use this tool in my day-to-day "real" life, I regularly pull it out of my back pocket to use on the set of *Jersey Shore*. If one of my roommates is flipping out or going through a particularly dramatic period, I try to offer positive advice, or at least a shoulder to cry on. A sensitive shoulder almost always helps the girls in the house feel better (Ron, Pauly, and Mike are cool to ask me for "Vinny wisdom," but you won't catch any of them cuddling up and crying into my hoodie), *and* it shuts down any negativity that might be clowning around in my own head. Lending a hand, figuratively and literally, always gives me a boost.

In fact, generosity might be the cheapest antidepressant on the market. I've read studies that say random acts of kindness strengthen our immune system and boost serotonin levels in our brain. Serotonin is linked to feelings like comfort, peace, and overall happiness, which is why most antidepressants work to stimulate the production of more of it. Elevated levels make us feel good! So when I say generosity takes your mind to a better place, I'm not kidding. Medical research proves it—helping others provides you with a natural high. Plus it doesn't stop there. Research also shows that the giver, the receiver, and anyone *observing* an act of generosity will *all* enjoy a natural serotonin bump. Triple score!

**HOLD UP**

# It Takes Work

The difference between taking an antidepressant and performing a random act of kindness is that one is a pill that you can quickly and easily pop into your mouth, while practicing generosity requires more work and effort. Personally, I don't like to take drugs, so practicing generosity is another natural tool I use to bump up my mood. That said, it takes dedication and a willingness on my part to *work* at feeling better. The same way making money takes work and losing weight takes work—for some people, being happy takes work. But I believe it's worth it; generosity is one of the best natural highs I've ever experienced.

---

Knowing this, it's not surprising that generosity, like a laugh attack, is highly contagious. Let's go back to the airplane scenario. I was on a six-hour flight from New York to Florida, and it was just one of those flights. The plane was packed with people, babies were screaming, and to top it off, some toolbag sitting next to me wanted to talk my ear off about *Jersey Shore*. If you look up FML (f*ck my life) in the dictionary, you would see a picture of me on this flight. An hour into the flight, it seemed like I was the only guy who wasn't chilled out on Xanax. I started obsessing about the metal tube I was stuck in, thirty-seven thousand feet up in the air. I started to sweat, I became dizzy, and my heart began pounding. Great—here we go again! This is when I decided to get my shit together and focus on something else.

I started talking to the super cute girl in the aisle across from me. She knew me from *Jersey Shore,* so we started bullshitting about where I was going and what my "real" life was like. I told her that I was going to host a party down in Florida, and it turned out that she lived in the town where I was headed. So here's what I did. I invited her to my party, and I told her to bring along a friend. At this point, I could tell that the dude sitting next to her was dying to get in on the conversation and the action, and I just sat back and waited to see how it would play out. What do you think happened next? Within a few minutes, the two of them started talking, and within the hour, I heard her inviting him to my event. Now everyone's in a better mood! I feel my stress level start to go down, and the plane ride finally begins to smooth out. To top it off, later that night, I saw both of them at my appearance hooking up in a corner.

I don't know for sure that the way this scene played out was directly influenced by what *I* did, but I like to think that my generosity had a contagious effect. I know that when I receive a gift of kindness, I feel good, and as a result, I want to pass those good feelings on.

Not only does generosity get you out of your head, but as an added bonus, your actions make other people feel good. Don't you appreciate it when someone is nice to you? Of course you do. So if you're still not buying it, let me assure you that being generous is not a wussy move. Making yourself of service to other people is one of the smoothest, coolest things you can do. It gives you *spiritual swagger*. People will notice and love you for it. Try it if you don't believe me.

## Spiritual Swagger

Swagger generally refers to how you walk, talk, carry, and present yourself to the world. To have "spiritual swagger" means you exude an attitude of cool, calm, and steady confidence. It means you have presence and are one hundred percent mindful of your surroundings, actions, and interactions with other people. Where does this "cool" attitude come from? Your inner power. Someone with spiritual swagger is totally disconnected from his or her ego and connected to his or her true self—a powerful force of pure, positive energy that's available to you at all times because it is *You*.

---

On a daily basis, I look for opportunities where I can be generous. I'm not necessarily talking about crazy gestures like building schools for kids in Afghanistan (although I applaud those who do), but simple things like helping someone across the street, loaning a friend a buck, or making somebody laugh. Practice your own version of generosity, and notice how it quiets your mind and puts you into a calm, cool, and drama-free mood.

**VINNY'S MENTAL WORKOUT**

## Be a Nice Guy (or Girl)

I encourage you to look for ways you can regularly be of service to your friends, colleagues, family members, and the random person you encounter. No need to go overboard; your actions can be small, and while what you "give" may seem small and silly, it can make a big difference. You see, some of the most valuable gifts aren't material. Being patient, giving someone your full-on attention, playing the peacemaker, and simply being kind and compassionate are huge gifts. And these are gifts that don't cost you a thing! For example, when I see that my mom's having a rough day, I tell her I love her. This takes me five seconds, and it makes her feel so good. While you're not always in a position to physically give, you can always be in a giving state of mind. Catch my drift?

For example, say some d-bag driver flips you off while you're trying to park your car, and you *don't* do it back. Instead you say to yourself, *I hope this angry douche has a better day*—that's an act of generosity. I'm not kidding; you're giving the gift of patience and compassion. Plus by choosing to react positively (which might not be your automatic reaction—your ego will encourage you to return the finger), you stop senseless drama from escalating and raising your stress level along with it.

Look for opportunities to give wherever you go. In every situation, ask yourself, *What's the best way I can help?* I think you'll be surprised to discover that when you focus on generosity, anxious thoughts and feelings of stress de-escalate.

Throughout the first season of *Jersey Shore*, I worked with a producer whose positive attitude alone was an act of generosity. As you probably know from watching the show, it's a stressful environment with negativity all over the place, so having someone on set who was always upbeat and who had the natural ability to see the humor in every crazy situation was a gift. And by *upbeat*, I don't mean in an annoying and fake kind of way. Her positive attitude was for real. When I was feeling particularly low, sometimes her smile was enough to pick me up and get me through the next several hours of shooting. (I sometimes felt like she was sprinkling positive fairy dust on me.) A smile sounds like a small thing, but it can have a huge effect on another person, and it's something you can give away freely *every day*.

## No Expectations

The secret to giving is expecting nothing in return. In other words—take more action than you get. I'm not going to lie: this will be a challenge for your ego, and also a great test. Your insecure ego likes to be stroked, applauded, and recognized, so as you practice generosity, ask yourself, *Am I expecting something in return? Do I want my efforts to be noticed? Do I still feel good about giving even if I don't get special attention for doing so?* Put your ego to the test; true generosity doesn't require a reward. Deepak Chopra makes this point in *The Seven Spiritual Laws of Success. What's in it for me?* is a question of the ego, whereas *How can I help?* is a question of the spirit.

For example, since making a name for myself as the kid who fist-pumps Seaside on *Jersey Shore,* I've also gotten involved in a lot of charitable work. I'm a spokesman for MTV's A Thin Line campaign, which works to prevent cyberbullying, and I've partnered with DoSomething.org to help facilitate antibullying initiatives in communities across the country. I'm also a supporter of the Love Is Louder initiative, which works to provide messages of love and hope to young people who feel they have no place to turn. Extending myself in this very public way is rewarding, and I'm grateful that I'm in a position where I can make a difference, but if I'm being honest—attaching my name to charitable causes and getting kudos for "doing good" strokes my ego to some degree. I have to be careful to keep my *self* out of it and stay focused on the cause. If thoughts start popping into my head like, *Vin—You're so awesome. You're so giving. Chicks are going to love you for all that you do,* I know that's my insecure ego talking, desperately trying once again to make me feel important on a surface level. You see, using a charitable act to one-up someone or to brag about your accomplishments isn't a true example of generosity; it's just a way to feed your ego. If you find yourself looking for props for being a good person, you're contradicting the practice of giving.

## HOLD UP

## What's Your Motivation?

Giving yourself props isn't necessarily a bad thing. Be proud of all of the things you do. Love yourself for what you do. Pride and self-love build your confidence, which is a good thing. Just be mindful of why you do what you do. What's your motivation? When it comes to being generous, be careful that your motivation is pure. If your actions are motivated by competition— doing good as a way to one-up someone else or as a way to make yourself *look* good—you're not practicing true generosity.

## True Generosity

The acts of generosity that are the most rewarding and the most effective for helping me to get out of my head and detached from my needy, greedy ego are the ones that often go unnoticed or unseen. For example, taking out the garbage or cleaning my house for my mom without being asked, showing love to a friend who's having a bad day, taking time to hang with and play video games with my little cousins. These things I do for no other reason than that I know they will help the person I'm doing them for feel better, and in doing them, I stop thinking about myself—what's making me anxious, worried, insecure, frustrated, or whatever. Generosity snaps me out of my head and connects me to my true self. Remember, all your whiny, bitchy thoughts aren't really you; they're just creations of your mind. Your true self is pure positive energy, and by doing right by others, you disconnect from your thoughts and *connect* to who you truly are.

It's interesting that most of the major religions of the world share a message similar to the one I'm talking about. For example, this prayer of Saint Francis of Assisi nails it:

> *Lord, make me an instrument of your peace.*
> *Where there is hatred, let me sow love.*
> *Where there is injury, pardon.*
> *Where there is doubt, faith.*
> *Where there is despair, hope.*
> *Where there is darkness, light.*
> *Where there is sadness, joy.*
>
> *O Divine Master, grant that I may not so much seek to be consoled,*
>     *as to console;*
> *to be understood, as to understand;*
> *to be loved, as to love.*
> *For it is in giving that we receive;*
> *it is in pardoning that we are pardoned;*
> *and it is in dying that we are born to Eternal Life.*
> *Amen.*

You don't have to be a Christian or "religious" in any way to appreciate what this prayer is all about—generosity is an act of spirit. It's your *true self* in action.

# Get What You Give

If you ask me, the most important role you can play in life is to be of service to other people. And the unexpected bonus is that when you give selflessly, you actually get many gifts in return. In other words—you get what you give. When I go out of my way to make someone feel important, heard, or respected, as a natural consequence they do the same for me. Now remember, true generosity isn't looking for a pat on the back or a handout, but when you invest in and make yourself available to other people, inevitably they will return the favor. It's just how the Law of Attraction works. The more you give, the bigger the payoff. Also, many of the spiritual gurus will tell you that by just *thinking* thoughts of kindness, love, peace, and success for other people, you'll attract all that good stuff into your own life.

By extending yourself to other people—through actions or just thoughts—and making generosity part of your daily MO, you will notice a support system begin to build up around you. This is so important. A support system—or what I call a "dream team" of people who love and support you unconditionally—is vital if you're feeling down. When I returned home after shooting seasons 1 and 5 of *Jersey Shore,* I felt completely broken and alone. I needed support, people I could lean on and trust, and my cousin Doug and my sister Antonella were there for me.

They'd both gone through their own garbage in the past (Doug had battled with addiction; my sister dealt with her own on again, off again anxiety), and I'd been there for them, so when it came my turn, they returned the favor. This is how generosity works. Extend yourself. Invest in and do right by people, and you will be rewarded in many ways.

# IN THE REAL WORLD: Generosity Is a Pimp Move

In the dating world, I've discovered that generosity is a "pimp" move. When I go out with a girl, I practice generosity by putting her first. If we're out at a club or a bar, before serving myself, I'll make sure to order her a drink. If her friends are along, I order drinks for them too. If we're in a crowded club or bar, I might also go out of my way to make sure everyone has a place to sit, even if that means I stand. At the end of the night, I take care of everyone's cab ride home. Basically, I look for opportunities to make her and her friends feel good. And why shouldn't I? Any girl I'm dating totally deserves it.

What's in it for me? When I'm attentive and of service in a dating situation, I become the *man*. Girls find me more attractive. No joke, by practicing true generosity, I've gotten some really amazing girls to like me who usually wouldn't have given me the time of day because of my "meathead" *Jersey Shore* image.

To be Krystal clear, in a dating situation, your "generous" actions must be genuine. Girls are super smart. They can sense in an instant if your generosity is real, so take my advice—do *not* use generosity as a play. Instead, be present—be real—be of service—and watch your love life jump to a whole new level.

Before moving on, I want to say a few more words about how serving other people has helped me, and in many ways *saved* me. As I've talked about, season 5 was a rough one for me. I was in serious crisis. I wasn't sleeping. I was physically sick, and there were moments when I was so anxious I thought I would pass out from all the crazy, negative adrenaline. Seriously, I really worried that I might not make it through to the end of the shooting schedule without having a major breakdown (which, I guess, I didn't). The one thing that helped me push through was writing this book and knowing that the message and tools that I'm giving you now might help you the way they helped me.

## IN THE REAL WORLD: Say Yes When Someone Asks for Help

Right before shooting began for season 2 of *Jersey Shore* in Miami, I hit another low point. I was nervous about leaving home to film again after what happened during season 1. The day that the production team came to film scenes of me at home in Staten Island before leaving for Miami, we hit a local bar where I regularly hang. During a break in shooting, the owner pulled me aside and asked if I'd be willing to head down the street with him and say hello to his daughter, who worked in a nearby shop. According to him, she was a big fan of the show, and he thought he'd surprise her with a drive-by from Vinny Guadagnino. I'd become friendly with this dude. He was always cool to me on Staten Island, and since I was on a break for a couple hours, I said, "Sure," and off we went.

What I didn't realize until we showed up at his daughter's hair salon is that he and his daughter hadn't spoken in over two years, and he was using me to help reunite them. It worked. I was the ideal middleman. I got them laughing and kidding around, and by the time we left, they'd made loose plans to see each other again. The bar owner thanked me for helping him reconnect with his daughter, and I thanked him for giving me an opportunity to be of service. The act of extending myself to another person instantly got me out of my own anxious head that day, and that's exactly what I needed.

While you may know me best as the class clown of the Shore, I honestly believe that true character is built through the selfless act of giving back. If you ask me, the most important role you can play in life is to be of service to other people.

## Moving On . . .

In the next chapter, "ABG—Always Be Grateful," I'll introduce you to the powerful and healing act of gratitude. I've found that in addition to generosity, when I focus on what I'm grateful for, much of the stress and anxiousness I'm carrying around surprisingly fades away. As with generosity, I'm talking about being grateful for small things, like your mom's home cooking or your dog sleeping at the end of your bed. Look around. There is always *something* to be grateful for.

# 8
## ABG

### ALWAYS BE GRATEFUL

I f you want to feel better about your life, try practicing gratitude. Being grateful means appreciating and accepting what you have today. This sounds simple enough, but most of us don't do this. How many people do you know who start their sentences with *"Once,"* as in "Once I get that promotion, my life will be better." "Once I'm driving my dream car, I'll be happy." "Once I move away from home, my problems will disappear." Or how about this one— *"All I need,"* as in "All I need to be happy is more money, a better job, a bigger house, and for so-and-so to fall in love with me." It's as if the dope life is just up ahead. Yet thinking this way is a trap, because *once* you get those things, what do you think happens? You want more, or rather, your *ego* wants more and will continue to insist that what you have is never enough.

If you find yourself dissatisfied and whining that your life is lacking in one way or another and obsessing about how happy you're going to be in the future when X, Y, or Z happens, realize that's your ego talking. Don't listen to it. Instead, smack some gratitude on its ass, and show it the door. Happiness is available to you *right here, right now* when you're grateful for, and accept, the life you have today.

In this chapter, "ABG—Always Be Grateful," I'll tell you what I know about:

- How gratitude will lift you out of a funk

- How to focus on the good, rather than the bad

- Why "acceptance" makes everything okay

- The difference between giving up and changing it up

- How to accept people and situations that make you crazy

## Look Around

Gratitude is another simple and amazing tool for combating negative, crazy thoughts and general feelings of anxiety and stress, because it's available to you at all times. You may not realize it, but you have the power to be grateful at any moment; all you have to do is look around. Even when life's got you down, there is always *something* to be grateful for.

When was the last time you felt grateful? If you can't think of a time, it's probably because you've unconsciously trained your mind to filter for the negative—that is, what's going wrong in your life rather than what's going right. Most everyone does this, so cut yourself some slack; you're not the only Debbie Downer at the party. Generally, people tend to focus on how they've been wronged, consumed with what's missing in their lives and obsessing over the life they wish they had rather than the one they've already got. Not only does this keg-half-empty way of thinking make you feel bad—wanting for more and feeling generally unsatisfied—but when you focus on your problems and how stressed you are, you only create more problems and more stress for yourself. Negative thoughts breed more negative thoughts, kinda like pop-up ads. You click on one ad, that one leads to another, and before you know it, you're stuck in a galaxy of irritating pop-ups. Your mind, just like your computer, can become quickly and easily contaminated.

Don't believe me? Then test this theory. For the next five minutes, concentrate fully on what's got you down today. That's right. Think about all the things that aren't right. Go ahead—let the negative thoughts run wild! And when the minutes are up, check in with how you feel. Do you feel better? Worse? The same?

My guess is that you feel even more stressed out and pissed off than you did five minutes ago. Am I right? Next, see what happens when you stop giving your problems so much of your time and energy. Focus instead on what's going right, and see how your mood improves.

## VINNY'S MENTAL WORKOUT

## Make a Gratitude List

While we were filming season 4 of *Jersey Shore* in Italy, there were many nights when mad arguments and high drama on the set got in the way of my getting a good night's sleep. I'd go to bed feeling stressed and anxious, and it'd be four in the morning and I'd still be awake, staring at a blank wall. In an effort to calm my nerves and get some Z's, I created a mental game in which I challenged myself to think of fifty things I was grateful for. I figured that if I redirected my focus to what was good in my life rather than the negative energy around me, I could eventually chill out and drop off.

I started with the big things, like *I'm grateful for my loving, caring mom; my thoughtful dad; my beautiful sister; my dogs Jelly, Dean, Alpha, and Xena, who are always there for me.* Next I listed everyday conveniences like *I'm grateful to have a roof over my head, a comfortable bed, and clothes on my back.*

Fifty is a high number, and I quickly started to run out of things I was grateful for. I really had to stretch my mind to come up with more positives. Soon enough, I was listing things that most people take for granted, like *I'm grateful for oxygen and water.*

This might sound kind of lame—who *isn't* grateful for oxygen?!—but my late-night experiment worked. By the time I reached number twenty-six (I think it was *I'm grateful for my arms and legs*), I'd successfully pushed all the negativity out of my head and replaced it with feel-good thoughts. Feeling gratitude allowed me to relax enough to nod off into a deep sleep—finally!

Making a gratitude list is essentially a redirection practice. You're retraining your mind to focus on the positive rather than the negative. This doesn't mean bad shit doesn't exist. Of course it does; practicing gratitude simply means you give the bulk of your attention to what's good versus what isn't. I'm not going to lie—this isn't always easy to do. At first, practicing gratitude will take one hundred percent of your concentration. Negative thoughts are powerful and often hard to ignore. I swear, it feels like it takes *triple* the number of positive thoughts to outweigh a single negative one. Still, it's worth the effort, because it works! As it turns out, positive and negative feelings cannot happen simultaneously.

The next time you're feeling anxious, stressed, or generally low-down, shift your thoughts to what's going well in your life, and make a mental list of what you're grateful for. If you're a visual person, you might try writing out a physical list. Write down everything you can think of that makes you smile or lifts your mood in any way. Remember, there's always *something* to be grateful for, and once you start thinking of things you're happy to have in your life, you'll likely start thinking of *more and more* things that you appreciate. That's just the way it works. Once you complete your list, check in with how you feel. My bet is that your grade-A nasty mood gets a positive lift.

# Appreciate Today

What I've discovered is that when I'm grateful for the big and small things that are going well in my life today, the negative chatter in my head stops making noise. Where before I may have felt all anxious and tense thinking "my life sucks" thoughts, once I focus on what I'm grateful for, I suddenly feel relaxed and calm. Why? Feeling grateful wakes you up to your life in the present moment, and when you focus your attention on what you're grateful for today, you cannot feel anxious, stressed, worried, or wanting for what you don't have. It just doesn't work! Try it. It simply cannot be done!

When you're focused on the right here, right now, your ego—the negative talk machine in your head—stops making noise. Remember, your ego lives in another time zone—tripping over the past and obsessing about the future, so when you're grateful for the moment, suddenly the bulk of your problems seem to magically disappear. As I mentioned before, your "problems" are most often about something that has *already* happened or about something that *may* happen in the days and weeks ahead. They're creations of the mind that don't exist in real time—meaning, they're not real. The only *real* thing is what's happening right now, so why not focus on what's going well today? My guess is that in this moment, you have more to be grateful for than you have to complain about.

Practicing gratitude has not only helped me to not dwell on negativity, but the more grateful I am, the better my life gets. All around, my life's gotten a positive bump—my personal relationships have gotten better, professional opportunities continue to come my way, and I feel and look better than I ever have. Bottom line—when you're grateful for what you have, you attract more of those things into your life. And, as an added benefit, if there's something you want more of, like money, fame, a new relationship, imagine having it now, feel grateful ahead of time for getting it, and—SHAZAM!— don't be surprised when it shows up at your front door. This is what's happened to me, and if it can happen for me, it can happen for you. That said, feeling grateful ahead of time is not the same thing as "wanting" something. You can't want what's already on the way. Get it?

## Accept When All Else Fails

So what if feeling good about your life and feeling grateful for what you have seem totally impossible? I understand that it's not easy to be grateful when you're feeling low. I've been there. This is when *acceptance* comes in especially handy; this is another mental tool I use all the time. To practice acceptance means you "accept" that sometimes things go wrong, situations don't always go the way you want them to, and while you may not like it or be happy about it, you accept that bad shit and difficult struggles are an inevitable part of life—and that when a struggle presents itself, there might actually be a good reason for it.

Acceptance clashes with our natural urge to want to run away, to hide from, or to fight against what's causing us pain. But resistance only creates more resistance, and the result is additional stress. Think about it—have you ever tried swimming against a current? It takes *a lot* of energy. It's exhausting, and you don't usually get very far, if you get anywhere at all. Trying to fight or control a shitty situation is just like this. It wears you down, plus it hardly ever works. Acceptance is when you stop swimming against the current and instead flip over on your back and let life carry you where it naturally wants to go. This may not be the direction you want it to go or think it *should* go. Acceptance includes trusting that there's a plan for your life that's beyond what you can understand or even imagine for yourself. The truth is that most people have a very limited perspective on the "big" picture. So, let go and let your life take its natural course, and when you do, you'll notice that much of your stress and anxiety *go* with it.

## Acceptance

Acceptance means you accept that people, situations, and events in your life are happening for a reason—yes, even when they feel superbly awful and make you miserable. Many spiritual teachers will tell you that there's a reason behind everything that comes your way. What's happening in your life, including the people in it, has a valuable lesson to teach you. When you look at it this way, it's easy to feel grateful for the people and situations that have shown up on your doorstep, because at the end of the day, they each serve a positive purpose—even when it's not obvious what that is!

---

I like the metaphor of acceptance and letting go so much I had it tattooed on my chest. (Maybe you remember the season 5 episode where I reveal my new big-ass tattoo to my roommates.) I'd always wanted ink on my chest, and after bottoming out and bailing during season 5 of *Jersey Shore,* I got the idea to have my favorite saying, "Let Go, Let God," tattooed right where I could see it. I thought, *This is exactly what I need to be reminded of every day.* These words remind me that there's a reason for everything. Instead of trying to control every detail of my life, if I just shrug my shoulders and "let go," I'll end up exactly where I'm supposed to be.

Letting go and accepting shitty situations is easier said than done. Honestly, it can be a real test, one I've personally struggled with, and yet I've come to the conclusion that there's a positive reason behind everything—depending on how you look at it. This is how I now view my battle with anxiety and depression. While it's caused me a lot of mental anguish and physical pain over the years, I've survived, and a lot of good has come from it as well. If it weren't for my chronic anxiety, I wouldn't have left college when I did and returned to Staten Island, where I eventually had to really hustle to finish out my degree (I did it in three and a half years while maintaining a 3.9 GPA). This is something I'm really proud of, and it might not have happened that way if I'd stayed at SUNY New Paltz. Another example—if it weren't for my anxiety rearing its ugly-ass head again during season 1 of *Jersey Shore,* I probably wouldn't have been so dead set on developing the triple-threat program that's saved me on more than a couple of occasions, and is (I hope) helping you now. In this respect, my struggle with anxiety has given me a positive purpose.

Reaching my breaking point at different times on and off the set of *Jersey Shore* forced me to go through a personal transformation that made me a stronger, more confident, and ultimately happier person. It was hell going through it, but now looking back, I recognize that the payoff was worth the pain. Every time I've struggled, my anxious mind has eventually led me in a positive direction, and for that, I'm grateful for all the times I've been knocked down.

Have you ever heard the expression "God won't give you more than you can handle"? (Remember: Don't get hung up on the words. For "God," you can substitute "Life," "the Universe," or whatever works for you.) It's another one of my favorite expressions, and I absolutely believe it to be true. I think that sometimes we're put in difficult situations that really test us but that we can ultimately handle. These situations force us to transform, like a snake shedding its skin, so that we grow stronger. In one of my favorite books, *The Road Less Traveled,* M. Scott Peck talks about how depression and other low-down moods are a "normal and basically healthy phenomenon . . . signaling that major change is required for successful and evolutionary adaptation." In other words, we often need a serious kick in the ass to become better versions of ourselves. These "kicks" can be 'effing painful, but if you can take a step back and trust that, ultimately, there's a positive reason behind every struggle and challenge you're presented with, and if you can *accept* this, the outcome suddenly becomes worth the temporary sting.

Every time I've been knocked down, I've ended up in a better place. Knowing this, I have faith that life is leading me exactly where I need to be.

## Sit in the Shit

So enough of the philosophical mumbo jumbo. You want to know how to "let go"? Good question. You let go of your shitty feelings by first allowing yourself to feel them. That's right—when I'm feeling particularly bad, I will literally sit down and force myself to feel my shitty feelings. For example, once after this girl I was dating and I split up, I laid down and concentrated on really feeling the sadness of missing her. Once I fully feel whatever it is—sadness, anger, frustration, jealousy, or heartbreak—I practice *accepting* the feelings and the situation I'm in rather than denying them, making excuses, or trying to run away and hide from them. I might say to myself, *Vinny, this is where you're at right now. Face it. Feel it. Be brave! As hard as it may be, trust that there's a good reason it's happening, and instead of resisting it,* accept *it.*

I'll be honest—the practice of letting go and accepting isn't the most fun. It can really suck. But what I've discovered is that the more I resist a situation or a feeling, the harder it bites me in the ass. By resisting, I end up creating more anxiety and stress for myself. When I notice negative thoughts and emotions dragging me down and instead accept the hand I've been dealt and trust that feeling better is not far away, my mood instantly lifts. For real, I start to feel better right away. I could be having the most stressed week of my life, but when I accept it, my stress level immediately starts to improve. Really—thoughts like *I accept that life feels really 'effing hard right now, but eventually I'll be okay* will instantly make you feel better. Relief comes from putting down the fight.

## BREAK IT DOWN

## Letting Go

When you "let go," you surrender to the fight. You might not realize it, but it's the fight that's causing you to have recurring stress and negative feelings. Why? Because you're fighting what *is,* and you can't fight against what's happening right here, right now without creating stress for yourself. It's a losing battle.

What's happening in your life might not be great. It could be terrible, but it's the only real thing you have. Accept where you're at, and choose to believe that there's a positive reason for whatever's shown up in your life today. Stop fighting what is and you'll notice that the stress in your body and mind begins to ease up.

---

There have been many times while filming *Jersey Shore* when I've felt anxious and around-the-clock crazy. I used to try to fight the shitty feelings by getting my drink on, retreating to another part of the house where I could hang alone, or walking off the Seaside set altogether. None of these moves *ever* worked. What did work was facing and *accepting* my shitty feelings. Once I pulled the tool of acceptance out of my back pocket, I'd feel relief. Not total and complete relief, but I'd feel noticeably better, and it happened instantly.

The kind of long-term stress that drags out and hangs around is what happens when you put up a fight, make lame excuses, or deny your feelings and the situation you're in. When you let yourself feel your crappy, painful feelings, you soon realize that avoiding them is more painful than it is to face them. You see, pain is actually fleeting; it doesn't stick around. Sure, the initial punch can knock you back, but once you steady yourself and start moving around the ring again, the pain begins to fade, and you realize you're okay; you're not broken.

## Change It Up

All this said, accepting your present situation isn't the same thing as throwing in the towel and *giving up*. If you're at all confused about this, let me be clear: I'm not suggesting that you stay in an unhealthy relationship, put up with a sketchy work environment, or let yourself continue to get beat up in school. Not at all. Acceptance doesn't mean you just suck up a *sucky* situation and not take steps to make it better. You can practice acceptance and also work toward changing it up. Case in point: Before leaving for Italy to shoot season 4 of *Jersey Shore,* I met a really cool girl. She was my type physically, and even better—she was cool on the inside too. No game playing, no drama—just a positive, nice person. For the first time in years, I'd met a woman who really sparked my interest, and she seemed to really be into me too. Unfortunately, we lived on opposite coasts, so we knew our dating days were numbered.

After spending an awesome week together in New York going to clubs, eating out, and just chilling low-key, we said good-bye. It really sucked! I felt myself being pulled into a funk where I could have easily hung out for weeks. But instead of going there, I made a conscious effort to practice acceptance. I told myself, *Vin—this girl is great, but your current work and shooting schedule, not to mention*

*your East Coast address, make dating her right now kind of impossible.*
I could have easily felt sorry for myself (and in fact, I spent several
days moping around and obsessing over when she was going to text
me again), but I ultimately decided to trust that the situation would
unfold the way it was supposed to, and I let go of my urge to control
the outcome. This doesn't mean I gave up on the relationship. Not
at all. I left for Italy with the intention of reconnecting when I returned Stateside, but in the moment, I accepted that we couldn't be
together.

So, what happened? I went to Italy and had my fun, and when I
came back to the States, we reconnected—as friends. Our relationship took a turn toward friendship, and as it turns out, that was the
right move. Friendship is working for us, and I don't regret a thing.
This outcome is one hundred percent better than the one that could
have been if I hadn't accepted the situation and then spent all my
time in Italy moping around and dwelling on how bummed I was
and texting her like a mad psychopath.

## Don't Give Up

Don't confuse acceptance with giving up. Giving up implies that you
can't make changes, and this just isn't true. You can totally take steps
to change any situation, but before you do so, you must feel your
shitty feelings and accept your situation in the present moment. Notice I said you need to *feel* your feelings, not let them *consume* you.
You must say to yourself, *This is where I'm at. This is how I feel.* Acknowledge the right here, right now, and accept it for what it is. Then
move on. Ask yourself, *Now what?* If you don't like your current situation and how it's making you feel, make plans and take action to
change it. Remember, you can't change the past or the future, but

you have absolute power to take positive action and make changes in the present moment. It's the present moment where all real change and action take place in your life. It's the only thing that exists! Ask yourself, *Is there anything I can do* right now *to change or improve my situation?* If the answer is yes, take action, son!

## IN THE REAL WORLD: Accepting the D-Bags

Not only does acceptance help you feel better about difficult situations, it helps you when dealing with difficult people. Whether it be a bully, your boss, ex-boyfriend or ex-girlfriend, or just some d-bag on the street causing you angst, your natural reaction may be to fight back, but realize you can take a different approach that will help shield you from negativity directed your way.

Instead of putting up a fight, if you choose instead to accept that you cannot control another person's actions, and understand that you have total control over your *own* actions and reactions, you can stop a fight before it spins out of control. How? By accepting that other people's negativity has nothing to do with you—it's their trip, not yours. As such, their negativity is not worth your time and energy. Don't react to it.

For real, there's no better way to fight back than to take a "Whatever, bro" attitude and put up your hands in acceptance. You may think that not reacting is a pushover move, but it's not. It's a power move! If you're not affected and drawn into a fight, guess who wins? You!

# Let It Go

Become aware of how you're feeling—tense, stressed, angry, sad, disappointed. While it's human nature to want to ignore, deny, or push away negative feelings and emotions, I want you to sit down and really feel them. Look, no one wants to feel pain. Feeling bad feels *bad,* and I don't know anyone who likes to feel bad. But put on a brave face and trust me on this one—feeling your shitty feelings is only temporary. Once you accept them, you can let them go.

Practice the following breathing technique that I borrowed from Zen monk Thich Nhat Hanh. Breathe in deeply while saying mentally or out loud, *It is what it is. I accept my current situation and the feelings that go along with it.* Next, slowly exhale and say, *I might not like it, but I trust that my life is happening the way it's supposed to. I'm letting go of my feelings of fear, anger, disappointment, tension, sadness, and grief.* Close your eyes and imagine yourself letting go of all the negative thoughts and feelings associated with your shitty situation.

Sometimes I do this breathing technique in combination with a walking meditation, or while doing yoga, and I visualize being out in the middle of a rough ocean hanging on to a buoy for my life. Then I imagine letting go of the buoy and letting the current carry me safely back to shore. Use this visualization or come up with your own, and once you've imagined letting go of your negative thoughts and feelings, ask yourself, *Now what? Is there anything I can do right now to change or make my current situation any better?* Be open to the answer, and when one becomes clear, take action right away.

If there's nothing you can do in the moment to change your situation, don't freak. The second you accept where you're at and admit to yourself that you don't know how to fix or resolve your particularly crappy situation, a very cool thing is likely to happen—a solution will often magically appear. No joke. When you let go of the negative thoughts and feelings you've been holding on to, you free your mind up for a positive solution to become clear. Be willing to say to yourself, *I don't know what to do here, but I trust that there is a solution and I will soon know what it is.* Before you know it, clarity will knock you upside the head.

## Moving On . . .

Generosity and gratitude act like the cleaning agent Formula 409 on your mind. They wipe away negativity so that positive thoughts can shine through. In the next chapter, "Flip the Switch," I explain how everything you've learned so far about letting go of crappy thoughts and feelings puts you in the perfect position to attract super cool people and sick experiences into your life on a daily basis. All it takes is shifting your thoughts from negative to positive, and when you do, good things will inevitably start happening to you. Trust.

# 9
# FLIP THE SWITCH

I'm an artist. I like to paint and draw. So when I visualize how negative thoughts block my mind, I picture a large black canvas. When I try to paint pink and red roses on it, I'm unable to see them over the dark background. But if I make the effort to remove all the black paint before I start and begin with a clean white canvas, then the roses I paint pop right off the background in vibrant pinks and reds.

Similarly, you may have a mind that's been painted black by your smack-talking ego, but underneath all the dark negativity is *You*, a pure white canvas. The mental workouts you've been learning up until now—how to wake up, hit the gym, eat clean, breathe deeply, and practice generosity and gratitude—are the keys to removing all that black buildup from your mind. Once your mind is wiped clean, so to speak, you can populate it with positive thoughts that will take root and bloom. I'm talking about creating better relationships, professional success, and personal happiness popping up in your day-to-day life. Are you into that?

In this chapter, "Flip the Switch," you'll focus on making positive thinking your ongoing mental workout, and as you do, prepare to see positive results. In addition, I'll tell you what I know about:

- How to flip negative thoughts upside down

- How to handle haters and bullies

- How to build a personal dream team around you

- How a positive attitude can change the world (I'm not kidding)

## The Upside to Being Upbeat

So much of my program is about shutting down your thoughts when they run off in a negative direction, but it doesn't stop there. Once you rid your mind of crazy thoughts, it's important that you replace them with positive ones. I'm not gonna lie, this is one of the hardest things to do. It's like walking straight up a mountain, and it's a workout I'm still sweating every day. If your mind, like mine, naturally runs dark, thinking positively is a practice that will require your full-on attention and focus, but I believe it's worth the effort. I've found that when I change my inner dialogue from negative to positive, the world changes around me. No joke. My on-set therapist, Dr. B, once explained it to me this way, "If you have an empty garden and you plant bad seeds, you won't grow any flowers. If you plant nothing, you'll just end up with weeds. But when you plant positive seeds, your garden will bloom." Trust me, your garden won't make it without planting positive seeds.

According to the Law of Attraction, what you think about the most is what shows up most often in your life. If you plant a bad seed in your mind, like *I'm a loser who can't ever land a good job,* you're going to *feel* like a loser who can't ever land a good job, and as long as you think and feel that way, that will probably be your reality too. We all know people who go from one bad job to another. They complain about rude-ass bosses, lame uniforms, and shitty pay over and over and over again. This is no coincidence. As long as they stay focused on working "loser" jobs, that's the only kind of employment opportunity that'll ever come their way.

The good news is that you can change your reality when you throw out the bad seeds and plant a few good ones. Wayne W. Dyer says in *The Power of Intention* that stress and anxiety are creations of the mind. They are "choices that we make to process events." Meaning, situations don't cause stress; it's how we process, handle, or *deal with* situations that causes stress. For example, if you discover that the twenty-seven onion rings you ate in a drunken frenzy last weekend put three extra pounds on your backside and you go crying to your bestie, "I'm fat. I'll never lose weight. No one will ever want to hook up with me," you're likely to feel bad about your body and your life. In a word: stressed. Do you see how that works? Your shitty *thoughts*—not the situation—caused you to feel unattractive and unlovable. Try replacing this negative noise with something more upbeat, like *I ate too many onion rings—whatever. I'm human. I make mistakes. One splurge won't ruin me; I still look good.*

I've been saying this all along—you have the power to change your reality by simply changing the running dialogue in your head. You're the conductor of the train. Switch tracks. Plant positive seeds, and then experience how your mind gains positive momentum.

## IN THE REAL WORLD: Attract a Better Reality

The Law of Attraction says that "like attracts like," so if you think negative thoughts, you attract negative experiences. My cousin Tommy is a prime example of this. He's the funniest guy you'll ever meet; his jokes will make you piss your pants, but he's negative beyond belief. Honestly, I've never known someone who talks about himself in such a miserable way. Not that Tommy doesn't have a few reasons to be down on himself—he's overweight, is out of shape, and has chronic back pain.

In his mind, he's broken, ugly, and fat. He even goes so far as to call himself a "fat ass," and he lets his low self-image limit what he can and can't do. He's always saying, "I can't do this, I can't do that, blah, blah, blah." For real, his negative thoughts are out of control. And guess what? His life never improves. He can never catch a break. He's divorced. He has no money. He eats poorly, and his physical condition keeps getting worse. I'm not kidding, the guy's a mess.

I try to tell him, "Hey, Tommy, you've got to stop saying and thinking such horrible things about yourself." If he only understood the Law of Attraction, that like attracts like, and if he chose to throw out the bad thoughts and replace them with good ones, like *I'm still young, I'm good looking and funny as hell,* his reality, and most definitely his attitude, would change for the better.

## Flip the Switch

I think we all know someone like my cousin Tommy, who can't seem to stop bringing himself down and automatically assuming the worst in every situation. Replacing negative thinking with positive thinking isn't easy, but it can be done, and the way to do this is to simply "flip the switch." Once you make a conscious decision to flip your shitty thoughts upside down, you can do so instantly—midstream, even. For example, say the thought is *I'm getting sick.* I hear people say this all the time. Every time you sneeze or your throat tickles, you think, *I'm getting sick,* and after thinking that for two or three days straight, guess what happens—you get sick! But if you were to flip that thought to *I'm feeling better* or shift your thoughts to something that makes you happy or that you're grateful for, you're less likely to become physically sick. No joke. There have been studies done that prove that positive thinking influences your physical health.

You'll find that almost as soon as you flip your mind switch, the better you'll feel both mentally and physically. All it takes is one positive thought before you notice an uptick in your mood, because it's *impossible* for you to think good thoughts and feel bad at the same time. It's just not gonna happen.

## VINNY'S MENTAL WORKOUT

## Squash the Bug

To flip the switch from negative to positive thoughts, you've got to first identify how you're feeling—sad, stressed, hurt, angry, disappointed, and so on. Once you name the feeling that's got you down, trace it back to the thought. Ask yourself, *What kind of thoughts are going through my head to make me feel so crappy?* For example, after I left the Seaside house during season 5 of *Jersey Shore,* I spent many days at home feeling scared, anxious, and weak. When I traced those feelings back to their crazy thoughts, I realized that I was playing the same few lines of negative dialogue over and over in my head. My internal sound track sounded like this: *Vin, you're never going to last if you return to the Shore. You're just going to break all over again. You're weak. You can't do it.*

Identifying the thoughts that are making you feel shitty is kind of like noticing a mosquito that has landed on you. Right before it has a chance to suck your blood and infect you, you pick it up by its wings and stare at it. Similarly, once you put your finger on the thoughts that threaten to negatively infect your mood, flip the switch (or squash the bug), and shift your thoughts to those that will make you feel better instead.

To do this, take a deep breath and focus on becoming present. Once your mind stops making noise and you're connected to *You,* your true, calm, cool, and chill self, ask, *What* positive *thought would make me feel better right now?* Focus on the thought or thoughts that'll lift you out of your funk. In many instances, thinking the positive opposite does the trick. For example, when it came to my decision to return to Seaside to finish out season 5 of *Jersey Shore,* I made a concentrated effort to replace my negative sound track with its positive opposite. I told myself over and over again, *I can do this. I have a family who is rooting for me. I am strong and brave. I have accomplished so much in my life. I can get through this, too. My struggle with anxiety is part of my path in life and I will push through, minute by minute.*

Let me give you another example of flipping the switch that most everyone can relate to: driving in traffic. Traffic can make me *really* crazy. It doesn't take much—road construction, someone cutting me off, a ridiculously long red light—before I notice my tension rising and my fists along with it. In these situations, I've gotten into the habit of checking in with the thought or thoughts that fuel my road rage. Recently, I realized that behind my anger was the thought *This traffic is going to make me late to my meeting, and I hate making people wait.* While this is a legit concern, sitting in traffic all stressed out and pissed off isn't going to get me to my appointment any faster. In moments of stress, a good question to always ask yourself is, *Is feeling bad going to make my situation any better?* The answer will always be—no! The only thing feeling bad accomplishes is making you feel *bad.* I have to remind myself of this when I get frustrated. Once I do, I'll make a conscious decision to flip the switch and change my thoughts from negative to positive. I'll think, *Vin, you may be late, and if you are, just apologize. No big deal. In the meantime, use this extra time in the car to breathe, settle down, and focus on all the points you want to bring up in the meeting, so that once you do arrive, you're super prepared to blow everyone away.*

### VINNY'S MENTAL WORKOUT

## Planting Seeds

Another mental workout you might also want to try is one that my therapist on the set of *Jersey Shore* recommended. Get in front of the mirror every day and talk yourself up. I know, this sounds kind of embarrassing, and maybe even fake. When Dr. B first suggested it to me, I rolled my eyes; I knew I wouldn't believe the positive crap I was telling myself. But after I forced myself to do it a couple of times, I discovered that it really does help, so I encourage you to give it a try.

Look at yourself in the mirror and instead of focusing on the negative aspects of yourself (which is what you probably most often do), focus on the positive. For example, if you struggle with your weight, instead of looking at yourself and seeing a fat kid and thinking all the crappy thoughts that go along with feeling fat, think about what you like about yourself, or what others like about you. You may say out loud (or think to yourself), *I'm a smart, caring person and a loyal friend.* Or you may choose to focus on the aspects of your life that are going well: *I have a pretty cool job and a shit-hot boyfriend.*

The goal of this workout is to replace your negative thoughts with positive ones *even if you don't believe them.* "You're planting positive seeds," Dr. B said. "Keep saying these things over and over to yourself." This will give your mind positive momentum. You're switching tracks and retraining your mind to focus on the positive, and eventually your mind will automatically go there.

As ridiculous as this exercise may seem, it's the one that has helped me the most. When I'm feeling overly anxious and stressed, I say to myself, *You will get through this. You are strong. You have happiness inside you always. You are already okay.* When I plant positive seeds, I'm almost always able to successfully flip the situation in my mind. And, if I'm already operating from a strong place, planting positive seeds helps to keep me rooted there.

---

Flipping negative thoughts upside down is a fun game to play, and the more you play it, the more your thoughts will start to naturally shift on their own. Sure, nasty thoughts are still going to enter your mind from time to time, but probably not as often, and when they do, they'll become easier to replace. Before long, your feel-good thoughts will outnumber the d-bag ones, and you may discover that you've become the cool, chill person everyone loves to be around.

## HOLD UP

# Suspicious Mind

Does all this talk about flipping the switch from negative to positive think-ing sound too good to be true? Are you calling bullshit? If so, what I can tell you is that when I think the worst—when I let my insecure, anxious, and fearful ego run the show—negative shit shows up in my life. Since that's the case, why wouldn't it work the other way around? Why wouldn't the same principle apply to being positive and upbeat? Ask yourself, *If I have the power to attract negative experiences, why wouldn't I have the power to attract positive ones?* Before knocking this idea down, give it a try. Flip the switch and then make your call.

---

Now, to be clear—the goal of flipping the switch isn't to com-pletely stop shitty thoughts from entering your mind. That's just not realistic. Plus the idea that you'd never have a negative thought again is kind of creepy, like something out of a sci-fi movie. The best you can hope for is to reduce their frequency. Changing your think-ing also doesn't mean you ignore reality. I've had people tell me that "thinking positively" is inappropriate and unrealistic when kids are committing suicide; people are losing their jobs, homes, and health care; and the threat of a terrorist attack is something we have to live with every day. While I fully acknowledge these threats, I believe it's okay to choose to feel good even when the world feels scary or as if it's falling apart around you. This doesn't make me, or you, an insensitive prick. Dwelling on the negative doesn't help or improve anything, plus it makes you feel bad. And *you* feeling bad only adds to the pile of already shitty things in the world.

# How to Handle Haters

How *you* choose to react in a situation is one thing, but what happens when you're surrounded by people whom you cannot control, and they're taking shots of high-octane hatorade? You know who I'm talking about—people who *negate* everything. You'll say something like "The Knicks are doing great," and they'll respond, "Yeah, but I bet they won't make it to the playoffs." You'll say, "I'm going to this sick club tonight," and they'll say, "Yeah, but none of the hot guys go there." These are people who have let their negative thoughts hijack their minds. If you're not careful, they'll hijack yours too. So I developed a mental workout I call "Negate the Hater"—to help squash other people's hate. Do you have someone in your life who's drinking the hatorade and bringing you down? If so, give this a try.

## Negate the Hater

On *Jersey Shore*, drama is the rule, and it's very easy to get pulled into a conversation where someone's talking mad trash. As tempting as it is, I never feel good about myself when I jump into a fight, so I've had to come up with strategies to counteract the negativity. For example, if I'm out with my roommates and everyone at the table starts bitching, I make a conscious decision to either stay out of it or attempt to flip the switch. How do I do this? Simply, I don't feed into the hate. I either keep my mouth shut or offer a positive counterpoint. The latter is more of a challenge, but it can also be a lot of fun when it works. Remember, the ego loves company, so the hater energy at the table tries very hard to pull me in, but as long as I stay positive, guess what happens? I often flip the mood. Now, that's

CONTROL THE CRAZY

power! When the ego no longer has an audience, it'll eventually stop making noise.

Another example—if one of my roommates is starting trouble, creating unnecessary drama, or just generally being a negative presence to be around, instead of focusing on how edgy he's making me feel and talking shit behind his back, I'll make an effort to be compassionate. I'll look at him like a dog that's been locked up too long in an animal shelter and think, *I'm sad for you that you're angry all the time.* My second line of defense is to notice what he's doing right. (This isn't always easy to do, but I've found that you can find the good in even the most annoying people if you look hard enough.) When I focus less on the negative and more on the positive personality traits of the people around me, I'm less likely to get sucked into their bad mood. Remember, controlling the crazy is all about controlling how you react. You have a choice in every situation. Instead of joining into drama, react positively, and you'll preserve the peace within yourself.

To be honest, flipping the switch isn't easy to do in a world filled with haters, gossip, and drama. My best advice is to keep in mind that you cannot change other people's actions and reactions—you only have control over yourself. Still, when you change *your* mood, you often influence those around you to change theirs. Now that's power.

# F*ck Bullies

I was bullied when I was in high school for being an awkward-looking kid in braces, so I know what it feels like to be a target. In particular, the hot, popular girls loved to hate on me. Once I was bullied by a girl who called me ugly in front of a bunch of her friends in the cafeteria. I think what she said was "You have a big, ugly f*cking nose." Back then, I didn't have all the tools I have now to flip her negativity upside down. While my first reaction was to yell back, "No it isn't, you stupid bitch," I just walked away. It was the best I could do to avoid a fight, but it was hard not to take her comments to heart and feel bad about myself as a result. In high school, I already felt like I didn't totally fit in, and being bullied only made it worse.

## IN THE REAL WORLD: Don't React

If someone says something ugly to you and you respond by saying something ugly back, you engage in conflict, and in most cases, you escalate the drama. It can be hard to resist the temptation to react to someone's nasty move online or offline, but the best defense in situations where someone is bullying you is *not* to react, or to react positively. People can't hurt you or bring you down unless you let them, so don't give them any ammo! Fighting negativity with negativity only creates more negativity. Period.

If someone writes or says something vicious about you, try not to take it personally. Don Miguel Ruiz says in *The Four Agreements* that by taking things personally, "you set yourself up to suffer for nothing." It's true. Bullies are ruled by their egos—the fearful voice inside their *own* heads. This voice is a master at stirring up insecurities, judgments, blame, anger, and a whole bunch of other garbage. Bullies are directing this negativity at you, but it's really *their* garbage. Catch my drift? Don't take on someone else's garbage. If you don't listen to or believe what bullies say about you, their words have no power. You shut bullies down when you don't take their words personally.

**HOLD UP**

# Speak Up!

Did you know that at least 160,000 kids skip school every week to avoid being bullied? Are you one of them? Do you know someone who is?

Often it feels like there's nothing you can do to stop the problem. But that's not true. It's easier than you may think. Research shows that when someone is getting bullied, either online or offline, if a bystander intervenes, the bully will back off within five to ten seconds. Yes, you read that right—it takes only a few seconds to scare off a hater!

What this means for you: If you know that a friend of yours or someone you know is getting bullied, speak up! Don't just sit back and watch it happen. You can put an end to a lot of hate simply by saying, "Yo—that ain't cool. Back off!" In the case of cyberbullying, consider leaving a comment that calls the bully out. By taking action, you can quickly put the haters in their place!

---

Now that I've become famous for my role on *Jersey Shore* and I'm in the celebrity spotlight, I have a new audience of haters. People tell me I suck, that I'm a sellout desperate for fame, that I have no self-respect, no family values, no brains, and that I'll never be taken seriously. I'm not going to lie—attacks like this can really bother me. They can feel like a punch in the face, but once I shake off the initial sting, I remind myself that what people say about me is their trip and has nothing to do with me. Wayne W. Dyer says in *The Power of Intention,* "That which offends you only weakens you," and I have to agree. When you get offended by something someone says or does, you are likely to react like a fool. Perhaps you remember a certain someone bashing his head into a cement wall when the drama-o-meter went into the red zone during season 4 of *Jersey Shore.* My advice? Remind yourself that whenever someone points a finger at you, they're really pointing it at themselves. Their hateful words are coming from a negative place inside themselves and really have nothing to do with you. Don't react. Instead, walk away, shut down your computer, disconnect, and disengage. If you can remember to take these steps, you will save yourself a lot of pain and suffering. Mahatma Gandhi wisely said, "Nobody can hurt me without my permission."

## Forgive the Hater

Your other line of defense against bullies or haters is to send positivity their way in the form of forgiveness. *God, forgive my haters for they know not what they do.* If this feels supremely hard for you, check in with your own desire to sling insults, win arguments, and come out on top—this is *your* defensive ego talking, egging you into a fight. Put down your boxing gloves and let go of your need to win. Slow down your aggressive thoughts, connect to your inner power, and practice forgiveness toward those who attempt to or actually cause you pain.

Forgiveness is one of the most powerful cleaning agents on the market. When you forgive people who have wronged you, what you're really doing is choosing not to be affected by their negative shit. Forgiveness wipes it all away. It can be super challenging to forgive. Not many people can pull it off—because most of us believe that forgiving people who've been hateful or vicious toward us means we're letting them off the hook in some way. My cousin Tommy believes this one hundred percent. I've seen him go after guys who do things as minor as swipe his parking spot unintentionally. He'll get out of his car, pump up his chest, and go after the guy. He thinks a "real man" gets angry and talks tough. Not true. Getting angry is easy. A real man is able to *let it go*.

Look, forgiveness isn't about giving people who have wronged you a free pass—you forgive so that *you* can move on. Bottom line— when you attach yourself to the pain that someone's caused you and become consumed with revenge or holding a grudge, the only thing you really accomplish is ensuring that you will continue to feel bad. Buddha says, "Holding on to anger is like grasping a hot coal with the intent of throwing it at someone else; you are the one who gets burned." Consider making forgiveness a regular mental workout. (And to all my tough guys out there thinking, *I'd rather crack his skull, bro!* check this—when you forgive someone, you win.)

## Squash the Beef

Holding grudges takes a lot of energy, and it never changes, fixes, or undoes anything; grudges and resentments only help you continue to feel bad. They're pointless! My advice? Squash the beef. Make a list of people you have legit problems with—big or small—and make amends with each one of them. Even if you feel you weren't in the wrong, say "I'm sorry" anyway. Squash it and move on. Each time you do this, you'll feel a little more at peace and better about *yourself*.

While forgiveness might not ever change someone else's behavior, it will change how you feel. Forgiveness shuts down feelings of hate inside yourself and boosts your mood. When you're in the forgiving mode, other people's negativity can't touch you. Forgiveness puts you back in control. You'll know you've forgiven someone when you no longer have an emotional reaction to what they say or do.

# Dream Team

Another one of the best defenses against negativity is to surround yourself with upbeat positive people. I have a group of select friends and family members I call my dream team. Each of them has a positive, calming effect on me, so I try to have one or all of them with me in situations where I feel my anxiety might be triggered.

Recently I brought a few of them along with me to Las Vegas to celebrate my twenty-fourth birthday. Imagine a master suite with a pool table and a dance floor, complimentary meals at the best restaurants, and gambling in the dopest hotels. Trust me—this was a sick time, but in addition to partying, I also had to work the red carpet, do a club appearance, and give several interviews. High-class problems, I know, but really—any one of these activities can trigger my anxiety big-time, so I had my dream team along with me to help keep me level, chill, and feeling good. Each one of them knows all about my struggle with anxiety, and so with my dream team around, I feel confident that if I do slip into a dark place, someone'll have my back. I can rely on them one hundred percent to help me feel grounded and safe.

My cousin Doug is on my dream team because he's someone who regularly flips negative situations upside down. Instead of focusing his attention on those who have wronged him, what's missing in his life, and how bad he may feel, he's one of the happiest guys I know. Yes, he has a bullshit commission sales job, lives out of a shoebox, and often has a hard time making ends meet. But you would never know it. He walks around with a smile on his face like he knows something that other people don't. And, in fact, he does. He's learned how to disconnect from his ego, and because of that, he's totally in control of his thoughts, his emotions, and his life. He may not look like much, but he's one of the most enviable guys I know.

## IN THE REAL WORLD: Create a Dream Team

It's so important to have a good support system of positive people around you when you're feeling down. My sister Antonella and my cousin Doug are a couple of my biggest supporters. They are there for me unconditionally in good times and bad, and for this reason I consider them gifts from God. I am so grateful to have them both in my life.

Who's on your dream team? Who's looking out for you? A family member? A close friend? Your therapist? Your dog? Know who these people (or animals) are, and be good to them. I'm serious—treat them well! Be there for them when they need you, and you'll discover that they're there for you in return. Hard times are made even harder when you're going through them alone. When you're feeling low, having a "dream team" in place can make all the difference in how quickly and successfully you're able to crawl out of the dark and start feeling good again.

I like to poke and tease him because he has this old-school pleather jacket he wears *everywhere*. He calls it his "uniform." We could be in Miami during the summer or in Canada in the fall, and Doug's wearing his pleather jacket either over a T-shirt or over a long-sleeved dress shirt. He changes it up so he doesn't look like a bum, but still I'll say, "Doug—you wearing that jacket again?" and he'll shrug and say in his super thick New York accent, "Yeah I'm wearin' it cause I look f*ckin' mint, bro!" He doesn't care about image or about what people might say about him. He's detached from all that. He's positively upbeat and lets his true, calm, cool self guide him in everything he does. I take him with me on tour and almost everywhere I go because he constantly makes me laugh. His energy is so uplifting; it rubs off on me. I call him my "pug." I just look at him and smile.

Finding people who give off good vibes is easy once you change your own internal dialogue from negative to positive, because you will simply attract them to you. Remember, like attracts like, so *be* the person you want to hang around. The truth is that you won't meet a lot of people who are cool, calm, and relaxed unless you're that way too. They just won't be drawn into your inner circle. You'll find that by practicing this program and making mindfulness, generosity, gratitude, and positive thinking your daily mental workouts, you will meet people who operate similarly.

Once I started practicing my program, I noticed that my circle of friends started to change. Drama-free people just started showing up in my life, from girls I was dating to new friends and people on my management team. It was as if, all of a sudden, positive people were drawn to me, as I was drawn to them—like we were surrounded by some positive force field. I realize how ironic this sounds, as someone who's made a name for myself on a show where finger pointing, misunderstandings, and arguments rule every episode. Yet in the real world, I've made a concentrated effort to cut out the drama in my life. I had to. Drama kicks my overanxious mind into high gear, so I've had to dial it down wherever I can. I stopped hanging out with friends who just sat around complaining about life or gossiping about other people. I also stopped paying attention to hateful comments about me on Facebook, Twitter, and other social media. I ignore people in the press who have nothing good to say.

Now some people just won't go away—like family. My cousin Tommy, who isn't the most upbeat guy you'll ever meet, who when asked how his day is going will almost *always* answer, "Terrible, bro," is still a major character in my life. And I want him to be! I just have to be careful how much time I spend around him. I love the guy, but sometimes I can't hang around him when he's in an especially dark mood or when I am. As I said earlier, you can't control other people, but you can control yourself, so I limit how much time I spend around people who have the potential to bring me down. By removing myself—this is how I take care of myself.

## IN THE REAL WORLD: Attract a Positive Crowd

Be choosy about who you hang around with. People who give off negative vibes are not healthy choices. Their energy will negatively affect you and most likely bring you down, whereas upbeat people will lift you up. Become the kind of person you want to hang around. Your positive energy will attract people who also give off a feel-good vibe, and before long, you'll have eliminated everyone in your life whose toxic energy messes with your head.

# The Big Picture

When you flip the switch, not only will you bring more positive relationships, situations, and events into your life, but your energy will rub off on those around you, bumping up the collective feel-good energy of the world. Bottom line: if we all thought positive thoughts, the world would be a better place. In one of my favorite books, *Conversations with God: An Uncommon Dialogue,* Neale Donald Walsch suggests that everything you think and do contributes to the collective consciousness. What does this mean? The way I interpret this idea is that we each have our individual brains and thoughts, and collectively we feed one big global brain that generates millions of trillions of thoughts.

Let's make up a number and say that 75 percent of the thinking minds on Earth are negative. That's a lot of negativity, and all you have to do is turn on the news to see examples of how this kind of thinking plays out in the real world: corporate greed, political corruption, racism, sexism, poverty, famine, and war. In other words, when the collective consciousness is negative, bad shit happens.

Now, what if we flipped that collective mindset upside down? Think about it. If everyone started practicing forgiveness, gratitude, generosity, and positive thinking, the world would be an amazing place, wouldn't it? People would feel good and treat one another fairly and humanely. There are some pockets in the world where this already exists. I hear Bali is one. I count Jamaica as another. While this little island has its share of poverty and sketchy politics, the people there are some of the happiest you'll ever meet. At least that's been my impression and experience every time I've visited there. The overall mood in Jamaica is calm and peaceful—and it feels amazing. Like Bob Marley said, "Don't worry about a thing. Every little thing, is gonna be all right." Imagine if that kind of feel-good vibe existed everywhere. The world would be transformed. For real, I believe we have the power to change everything if only we collectively thought positively. You think I'm crazy? Is this idea too far-fetched? I choose to believe it's possible.

## Moving On . . .

So now that I've given you all the tools in my toolbox, it's up to you to use them. In the next and final chapter of the program, "Maintain," we'll put it all together by reviewing everything you've learned over the past nine chapters to create a mix-and-match program to control *your* crazy.

# 10
# MAINTAIN

**W**hen it comes to maintaining my program for battling anxiety, low-down feelings, and everyday stress, I've figured out what combination of tools works best for me, and that's what I use. I approach my mental health the same way I do my gym workouts—I switch it up. I may focus on my abs one day and my chest and arms the next, but nearly every day, I do *something*. When it comes to keeping my mind in shape, I follow the same rules. I vary the tools I use, but every day I do something to control the crazy and maintain the connection to my cool, calm, and steady self.

For example, on Monday, I might tackle my anxiety on a mind and physical level by taking a long, meditative walk around my hood. On Tuesday, I may attack it on a spirit level and spend a few minutes adding to my gratitude list, and nearly *every day,* I make time to hit the gym, eat stress-free foods, and help someone out. What I do really depends on the situations I find myself in and my mood. I keep myself in check by "checking in" at different times throughout every day. I'll take a look at the people around me—are they giving off a feel-good vibe or stirring it up and creating drama? I'll grade the environment I'm in—is it upbeat or bringing me down? Then I'll check in with where I land on the Negativity-o-Meter. Am I at a 5 (in a dark place) or at a 1 (pretty peaceful and chill) or somewhere in between? If I discover that I've wandered into a "my life sucks" dark place, I'll immediately pull a tool or two out of my back pocket to help me disconnect from my shitty thoughts and reconnect me to my pure and positive "true" self.

You should approach your mental workouts the same way—mix it up, but commit to doing something every day. The cool thing about my program is that there are many tools to pick from. And there's no right or wrong way to mix them up. Do what works for you.

In this chapter, "Maintain," I'll tell you what I know about:

- How to mix and match tools in a variety of real-life situations

- The downfall of becoming "spiritually cocky"

- What happens when you fall off the program

- The secret to controlling the crazy long-term

## Mix It Up

To give you an idea of how to mix and match various tools, I've listed some very common, everyday situations that will more than likely pop up in your life in the days and weeks ahead. Then I suggest how you might attack each one on a mind, body, and spirit level. There's really no right or wrong way to attack these situations. Experiment. Play around. You're going to figure out which tools work best for you and how often you need to use them. If one doesn't work, try another. If one works especially well, use it often. (And in case you've forgotten these mental workouts already, I've listed the page numbers where they appear.)

## You're Hoping to Kill It in a High-Pressure Situation

*Try this: Eat clean (pages 115, 121). Practice mindful breathing (pages 140, 183). Call out negative thoughts (pages 62, 66, 183, 189).*

Let's say you're feeling nervous, tense, or anxious about an upcoming test, a job interview, or an important meeting. You're freaking out. What do you do?

For starters, before heading into any of these situations, make sure you eat clean. "Stress-free" foods like lean proteins, whole grains, fresh fruits, and vegetables work *for* you. They level your head, whereas caffeine and sugar can shift an anxious mind into high gear. For this reason, I strongly suggest you lay off the double espresso and crumb cake before heading into any high-pressure situation.

Next, practice "mindful" breathing. Mindful, focused breathing is one of the most powerful tools for relaxing and quieting the mind (that is, killing stressful thoughts), plus you can do it anytime, anywhere. So, before walking into a high-stress situation, make time to breathe—while you're getting dressed, driving your car, in the elevator, sitting in the waiting room, wherever! As you focus on your breath, you'll focus less on your anxious *I'm going to mess this up* thoughts.

Finally, anytime negative, sabotaging thoughts creep back into your head, throwing you off focus either before or during your test, meeting, or interview, remember to question the voice behind the thought. Call it out! Remember, thoughts like *I can't* and *I suck* are just the senseless talk of your ego. Don't listen to it. It's not real. Tap into *You,* and take back control.

## You've Got a Food and Drink Hangover

*Try this: Hit the gym (page 97). Eat clean (page 115, 121, 132). Check yourself before you wreck yourself (pages 107, 112).*

Let's say you went out to the clubs, or maybe you hit your favorite bars and had a few too many. Then you joined some friends for greasy after-hours diner food. The next morning, you wake up feeling like crap. You feel both physically and mentally shot. What do you do?

The alcohol has dehydrated you, so you might want to start your recovery by pouring yourself a big glass of water. Remember, dehydration can lead to an increase in anxiety, nervousness, stress, and fatigue. Once you finish that glass, pour yourself another.

Next, drag yourself to the gym, or do *something* physical. Get outside, and take a simple walk around the block. Do a half-ass workout in your living room. Just get moving. If you don't feel good physically, you're not going to feel good mentally, so even if working out sounds like the last thing in the world you want to do, do it anyway. It'll make you feel better—guaranteed.

Finally, make a mental note of how much you drank the night before and what you ate that knocked you down so hard, so the next time you go out, you're fully aware of what you can handle. By all means, have fun, but check yourself before you wreck yourself. Understand your boundaries. By taking care of your physical health, you preserve your mental health. Truth.

## You're Trying to Pick Up a Girl or a Guy

*Try this: Check your ego (pages 33, 45, 47, 63). Get present (pages 79, 86). Tap in to your inner power. (page 58).*

Let's say you've got your eye on someone, but you're convinced they're out of your league. You want to make a move, but you're nervous. You're afraid you'll say something stupid or act like a lunatic. My advice?

Act like a dog. Remember, dogs are the perfect role models because they don't think. They have no ego. They're cool and calm and give off a nonthreatening vibe. So before you approach someone, check your insecure ego at the door by taking a few minutes to focus on your breathing. Breathing will help to calm any anxious thoughts swirling around in your head. I do this all the time when I'm in the club environment. I'll take a step outside and slowly begin to breathe. It's a super subtle move; no one knows what I'm doing, and yet a few deep breaths will quiet my mind and help me tap into my inner cool.

Once you've done that, walk up to whoever you're into and focus all your attention on them. Nine times out of ten, this will draw him or her right in (and you know what that means—*hook up!*).

If your nerves are *still* getting the best of you and you're standing there stuttering and making idiot small talk, remind yourself that underneath our social costumes—the stuff we wear on the outside— everyone's made of the same stuff *on the inside*—pure, positive light and energy. So if your ego's trying to convince you that he or she's too good for you, or that someone else in the club stands a better chance of hooking up with this hottie, turn the voice down. It's talking nonsense. On a spirit level, we're all the same. This means that it's an equal playing field. Get in there and make a play.

## You're Sweating the Small Shit, like Sitting in Traffic

*Try this: Track your feelings back to the original thought (page 189). Flip the switch (page 188). Practice gratitude (pages 159, 169).*

Let's say you're having negative knee-jerk reactions to the small shit, like honking your horn and screaming "Hey, asshole" at the guy who just cut in front of you on the freeway. Before you take your hostility a step further and ram into the back of his car, put your feelings in check. Remember, your emotions are triggered by your thoughts, so ask yourself, *What thoughts are setting me off?* You can trace any emotion you have back to its original thought.

Once you put a finger on the aggravated thoughts that are causing *you* to behave like the A-hole, practice flipping the switch. Take a deep breath and ask yourself, *What* positive *thought would make me feel better right now?* If you can't think of anything positive, focus on what you're grateful for. When you're grateful for the big and small things that are going well in your life today, the A-hole voice in your head will stop making noise. Why? Feeling grateful wakes you up to your life in the moment, and when you focus your attention on what you're grateful for *right here, right now,* you cannot feel angry, irritated, and pissed off at the world around you. The two cannot happen at the same time.

## You're Bummed Because Your Girlfriend or Boyfriend Broke Up with You

*Try this: Feel your shitty feelings (page 178).*
*Practice acceptance (pages 174, 179, 183).*

Let's say you're feeling really bad because your girlfriend or boyfriend just broke up with you (and by text—what a douche). How do you get over it?

Feeling better begins with your allowing yourself to fully feel your shitty feelings. I'm not gonna lie—this is no fun, but as soon as you do it, you'll start to feel better. Once you've faced whatever it is—sadness, anger, frustration, jealousy, or heartbreak—trust that there's a good reason things went down the way that they did, and instead of trying to fight your reality, *accept* it. Remember, to practice acceptance means you "accept" that sometimes things go wrong, but that there might actually be a good reason for it. In this case, the guy or girl you were dating was probably not right for you. Thank the universe for intervening and saving you before the relationship took a major nosedive!

Acceptance includes trusting that there's a plan for your life that's beyond what you can understand or even imagine for yourself. If you're fighting this truth by stalking the guy or girl who just broke up with you—stop. What's done is done. Let go, and when you do, you'll notice that much of your stress and heartache *goes* with it.

## You're Obsessing over Your Weight Problem

*Try this: Flip the switch from negative to positive (pages 33, 189).*
*Practice gratitude (pages 169, 171).*

Let's say you're feeling bad about your weight. You can't stop comparing yourself with others and feeling like you'll never fit in. What will make you feel better?

Remember, your ego has you believing that who *You* are is what you have, who you know, how you dress, and what you weigh. Don't listen to it. The negative noise in your head is not your *true* voice. It's not *You;* it's simply your mind running wild, and you have a choice as to whether you want to listen to the wild rant, and also what to believe. Just because your mind has said something about you, like

*I'm unlovable, unattractive and I'll never fit in,* doesn't make it true. Remember, *You* are so much more than what goes through your head. It's just that you've been listening to your critical ego for so long that you've lost touch with your true self—*You* are as lovable, as beautiful, and as worthy as anybody else.

That said, I know how bad it can feel when you feel like an outsider—it sucks! So, if peer pressure's got you down, try flipping the switch. Get in front of the mirror, and instead of focusing on what you *don't* like about yourself, focus on the things you do like (or that other people like about you), and feel gratitude for the things that are going right in your life. Remember, there's always *something* to be grateful for. All it takes is one grateful thought before you notice an uptick in your mood, because it's impossible for you to think grateful thoughts and feel bad about your life at the same time.

If feeling positive and grateful still isn't working for you, ask yourself, *How much of my identity is wrapped up in my "problem"?* Remember, *You* are not your weight problem. *You* are so much more than the "fat girl." Stop giving your problems so much of your energy, focus, and power. Your true power comes from within.

## You Wake Up Every Morning with a Stress Headache

*Try this: Hit the gym (page 97). Improve your sleep (page 109). Flip the switch (pages 189, 191).*

Let's say you wake up every morning with a stress headache, along with tightness and tension in other parts of your body as well. Where's the relief?

Remember that negative thoughts trigger negative emotions that often manifest as physical pain, stress, and tension in your body. You can work out the outward signs of your inner stress through high-intensity exercise. For real, this is one of the best ways to relieve a stress headache, anxious stomach, racy heart, and tense shoulders.

Plus exercise also helps you get a good night's rest. Remember, if you don't get enough Z's, you set yourself up for mental warfare. If you're waking up with a stress headache, maybe you're not getting enough sleep. Six to eight hours is what doctors recommend, and I'd have to agree. I know firsthand that slacking on rest will shift your energy into low gear, along with your mood.

And, finally, change the way you're thinking. If every time you open your eyes, you think, *I'm so stressed,* flip the switch. Tell yourself, *I'm feeling better.* Even if you don't *feel* that way, say it anyway. Planting positive seeds will give your mind positive momentum. By switching gears, you retrain your mind to focus on how good you feel, and as a result, you will start to feel physically better.

## You Hate Your Shitty Job

*Try this: Practice acceptance (pages 174, 183, 191). Look for changes you can make—today (page 62). Disassociate from your problem (page 79).*

Let's say you're stuck in a dead-end job, and it's putting you in the kind of bad mood that's affecting your friendships and relationships. To put it bluntly, you're becoming a real pain in the ass to hang around. What should you do?

Accept where you're at. Practice saying mentally or out loud, *It is what it is. I accept my current situation and the crappy feelings that go along with it.* Fully feel your feelings of anger, disappointment, tension, and frustration, and then imagine letting go of them. Once you imagine yourself "letting go" of all the negative thoughts and feelings associated with your job, ask yourself, *Now what? Is there anything I can do right now—as in* today*—to make my job situation any better?* Remember, acceptance doesn't mean you just suck up a *sucky* situation and don't take steps to make it better. Once you accept where you're at, look for ways that you can change your situation right now, and then take action. Maybe you can make a goal to apply for three new jobs before the end of the week. Remember, it's only in the present moment that you can change your life.

If no solution comes to mind, ask yourself, *How attached am I to my shitty job?* Remember, when you hold on to your problems and let them consume you—in this case, obsessing over how much you hate your job—you end up with more of the same: one dissatisfying shit job after another. Also, when you identify yourself with your problems—"I'm the guy who has a lousy job"—you continue to *be* the guy with the lousy job. See what happens when you stop giving your problems so much of your time and energy. Remember, your "problems" are not who *You* are.

## You Can't Focus on Your Game

*Try this: Minimize distractions (pages 75, 82). Breathe (pages 63, 140). Get present and tap in to your inner power. (page 58).*

Let's say you're having a hard time focusing on your game. This could be in the classroom, on the field, out at the clubs, or on the job. If, for example, your college professor has just asked you to brainstorm some ideas for an upcoming assignment and you're stumped, what can you do?

The first thing I suggest is to cut down on whatever techy distractions you have going on around you. Remember, when you become consumed by the TV, Internet, or texting, you allow your mind to wander into another time zone—the past or the future. And when you're somewhere else, you can't focus on what's right in front of you. In this case—your assignment!

Once you've removed any and all obvious distractions, breathe. Mindful, focused breathing will quiet your mind—the one that loves to overanalyze and judge, the one that says, *You're gonna bomb this assignment, bro.* As soon as you turn down the noise, you'll find that you wake up to the present moment. Once you're connected, you're in a much stronger position to focus on the job at hand, get shit done, and kick serious ass. I've found only when my mind is turned off can I really get into my "zone."

## You're Faced with Your Biggest Fear

*Try this: Disassociate from your fear (pages 79, 90). Breathe (pages 63, 140). Practice generosity (pages 154, 159).*

Let's say you have to confront your biggest fear: public speaking, getting your blood drawn, jamming into a crowded subway car, overlooking a cliff, whatever. I've already told you what my biggest fear is—flying. How do you face yours?

Become aware of fearful thoughts and then try disassociating from them. When fear starts to take you over, say to yourself, *Here they come again—another string of stupid thoughts trying to take over my mind, my emotions, my reactions, and actions.* Remember, fear is just your mind running wild, and you can choose to believe the wild, crazy thoughts that'll spin you emotionally (in my case, *I'm going to crash and burn on this plane*) or not.

Next, practice focused breathing. What's so cool about mindful breathing when you're freaking out is that when you maintain a steady, calm breath, your brain gets the signal from your body that everything is okay. In situations where your fear and anxiety have begun to spin out of control, practice focused breathing to shift your mind down from hyperdrive to low gear. It's really amazing how this works!

To further calm your nerves, practice generosity. Help someone out. Be of service to another person. No need to go overboard; your actions can be small. When you're selfless, you're focused on yourself *less*. So when fear-based thoughts ramp up, practice generosity to redirect your energy and attention. Before you know it, you'll have forgotten what you were so afraid of (at least, temporarily).

## You're Ready to Put Resentments to Bed and Make Amends

*Try this: Forgive (pages 164, 199). Practice acceptance (pages 174, 183).*

Let's say you and your bestie had a falling out. You haven't spoken in months, and every time you think about the stupid argument that got in the way of your friendship, you're overcome with feelings of sadness, anger, and general stress. You're tired of feeling this way; you're ready to put resentments to bed and make amends. What do you do?

Whatever your friend did to piss you off, forgive her. This can be super challenging, but when you forgive people who have wronged you, what you're really doing is choosing not to be affected by their negative shit. In other words, you win. Making amends and saying "I'm sorry" is a master play. It helps you to feel better.

*If* your friend doesn't accept your apology and continues to hold on to her grudge, practice acceptance. Your friend's attitude has nothing to do with you—it's her trip, not yours. As hard as it may be, don't react to it, because if you do, the fight between the two of you will only continue—guaranteed. Instead, maintain a chill and peaceful attitude. Remember, you cannot change other people's actions and reactions—you only have control over yourself. And here's the kicker: when you change *your* mood, you often influence those around you to change theirs. Continue to keep the peace, and your friend just might come around.

## You're Future-Trippin' over Something That Hasn't Happened Yet

*Try this: Get real (pages 47, 73, 79). Practice acceptance (pages 174, 183). Hit the gym (pages 97, 107).*

Let's say you're anxious about hearing back from the college you're hoping to get into, the hiring manager at the company where you recently applied for a job, or the guy or girl you gave your number to the other night. You're future-trippin', and your anxiety is spinning out of control. What can you do to chill out?

Realize that right now is the only real thing. Remember, the past and the future don't exist, which means you cannot control them. In other words, your obsessing over the future will change nothing. It will only create stress in your body and your mind. So chill. Accept that things will happen as they should, and let go of trying to control the future, because you can't.

If chillin' feels impossible to do, try slowing down your anxious mind by listening to the silence in between your thoughts. Remember, when you listen to what *isn't* there versus what *is* there, your future-trippin' ego will eventually stop talking shit. And once your ego is no longer making noise, feelings of anxiousness, stress, and general negativity will quiet down too.

Finally, go get some physical exercise. Hit the gym to get your mind off of what's consuming you. When you focus on moving, stretching, and pushing your body to its physical limit, you snap yourself into the right here, right now, and you can no longer fixate on the future.

## You're Getting Roped into Hater Drama

*Try this: Stay positive (pages 65, 186). Breathe (pages 63, 140). Surround yourself with upbeat positive people (pages 194, 200).*

Let's say a group of your colleagues or classmates are stirring it up and trying to drag you into drama. It's tempting to jump in, but you really don't want to get involved. What do you do?

I totally get this one. On *Jersey Shore,* it's very easy to get pulled into conversations where someone's talking mad trash. As tempting as it is, resist! Keep your mouth shut, offer a positive counterpoint, or walk away. Remember, the ego loves company, so the hater energy in the room will try very hard to rope you in. But as long as you stay positive, their bullshit can't touch you, and in some cases, your positive attitude might just flip the mood.

If you find this easier said than done, take a breather. A few deep breaths might be all you need to clear your head when negative thoughts and emotions are triggered inside you. By taking a breather, you just might stop an ugly situation from getting uglier. Remember, mindful breathing wakes you up to the *right here, right now,* where you can connect with your inner power—the steady calm within you that's immune to hater drama.

And, finally, remember that one of the best defenses against people drinking the hatorade is to cut them out of your life and to surround yourself with fun-loving, upbeat people. The best way to do this is by changing your internal dialogue from negative to positive. Like attracts like, so be the positive person you want to hang around, and you'll attract upbeat people to you, like bees to honey, while the haters will quickly lose interest in you.

## Spiritually Cocky

As you get better and better at shutting down negativity and controlling the crazy, beware of becoming "spiritually cocky." This is something I've been personally challenged by. The truth is that once you start feeling better about yourself, you may feel like you have an edge on life and an advantage over other people who don't know how to tackle negativity like you do. Before you know it, you may catch yourself feeling, and acting, pretty cocky.

For example, after wrapping season 5 of *Jersey Shore,* I returned home to Staten Island and jumped right back into practicing my program and writing this book. After several weeks of hitting the gym, eating clean, practicing mindfulness, and being present, I felt like my anxiety and depression were back under control. I was feeling confident again—enjoying my fame, my money, and the celebrity lifestyle. I was feeling above it all—like nothing could touch me.

The next thing I know, along comes another great girl (seriously, I fall in love every other week). And this girl made me feel really special. We hung out nonstop for two weeks. Everything was clicking, and then we had this petty argument, and she stopped talking to me. Just like that, she turned on me and cut me out of her life. I was crushed, sad, and pissed! She really messed with my head. After a few days of moping around like a little bitch, obsessed with thoughts like *How did this happen? Why doesn't she like me anymore?* I understood the lesson this girl had inadvertently given me. I'd become spiritually cocky, like I was a supreme being, immune to pain and hardship. Who did I think I was—some kind of superhero?

## BREAK IT DOWN

# Spiritually Cocky

After you've been practicing this program and using these tools for a while, you're going to start feeling really good. In fact, you might feel so good that you convince yourself that you're invincible and that you have an advantage over other people who don't know how to control the crazy like you do. It's easy to get cocky when you're feeling on top. Just beware that you're not immune to the occasional knockdown. Life will continue to throw you punches—guaranteed. And when it does, use the tools you've learned throughout these pages to wipe yourself up off the floor and get back in the game.

---

Of course, I'm not a superhero, and this girl reminded me how very human I am. I'll never be immune to suffering. Fame, money, and success will never change that. People and situations will continue to test me and cut me back down to reality. Doing the mental workouts and practicing my program give me an edge, but life is still going to throw me punches—without a doubt. That's just the way life is, and in fact, the occasional jab is how we're tested. Without bad days, you would never know what *You* are really made out of. I believe one hundred percent that you, I—everyone—needs the occasional challenge and setback in order to grow stronger. That's the point of life, isn't it? To continue to become better and more badass versions of ourselves. This is what personal evolution is all about. True, sometimes the challenges and setbacks we face are painful, but they're all important and meaningful because we can learn and grow from them.

I believe that people and experiences enter our lives to teach us things we need to learn at the exact moment we need to learn them. So when challenges present themselves to you in the future, instead of letting them break you, remember to *accept* them. Feel grateful for them, and welcome them as opportunities to bounce back even stronger.

In the days and weeks ahead, don't be surprised if it's when you're feeling spiritually cocky that life decides to throw you a punch. No need to freak out! You can handle it, because you now have the tools to control the crazy, put negativity in check, and get back in the ring. Yes, you may feel like you've been beaten up, but always remember this—no one and nothing can break you.

## Falling Off

Just the other night I woke up out of a sound sleep. My heart was racing, and my head was full of anxious thoughts. I'd had a bad dream—*you know,* the kind that feels really real. I'd dreamt that one of my uncles had died. In the dream, I was attending his funeral, and when I woke up, I had a really hard time shaking how sad I felt, so I sat up in bed and took a few deep breaths. I know myself well; if I don't take immediate action to stop it in its tracks, my anxiety can spin out of control. I quickly got out of bed and walked over to my open window, looked out at the night, and focused on quieting my mind and becoming present. I told myself, *Vinny, don't fall sucker to your negative thoughts. That's just your mind running wild; it's not* You. I practiced a combination of mindful breathing and observing my thoughts as separate from who I am. As I focused on the silence in between my thoughts, I connected to the cool, calm, steady power inside me that says, *In this moment, you're totally okay.* After a few minutes, my anxiety was gone, almost like it had faded into the darkness of the night. I went back to bed. The next morning, I made a point to eat a super charged, healthy breakfast and headed straight to the gym. By midmorning, I was back in control of my mind, body, and spirit.

Just like I did, if you feel your mind racing and ramping up and your emotions start to spin, don't sweat it. Even if you totally fall off the program, you have the tools to get right back to it.

Plus, if I can be philosophical for a moment here, you can never *really* fall off the program. *Falling off, failing,* and *f\*cking up* are words that the ego—the critical voice in your head—uses. Don't listen to it. Just as the sky returns to a calm, clear blue after a thunderstorm rumbles through or the ocean becomes steady again after a tsunami, *You* always remain *You*. Life situations and people will threaten to shake you up, but they can't break *You*. In this respect, *You* can never really fail. When in doubt, practice everything you've read in these pages. Get real. Wake up. Exercise. Eat clean. Breathe. Practice generosity and gratitude. Replace your negative thoughts with positive ones. This is how to maintain your connection to the cool, calm, and steady power that's within you at all times because it is *You*.

# Hustle

Maintaining the connection isn't always going to be easy. You've got to keep at it. You've got to hustle. In *The Road Less Traveled,* M. Scott Peck says that "life is difficult" and personal growth is a "complex, arduous and lifelong task." I have to agree. You can't think positive for two days and expect your life to be all put back together. Not so fast. You have to be upbeat for *two months,* day in and day out, before you can expect to start to see changes. It takes time. It takes effort.

If you don't hit the gym, you run the risk of getting fat. It's the same with your mind: if you don't put your muscle into maintaining a positive mind, you run the risk of becoming consumed and messed up by stressed-out, 'effed-up thoughts. In other words: you get out what you put in.

Maintenance requires work, and I'll be honest—it's *hard* work. I know this better than anyone. It requires your constant presence. I have to remind myself of this all the time. It's so much easier to be negative. I swear, it's like human beings are addicted to stress and drama. Our minds just naturally seem to want to *go there*.

A trick I use to help me from "going there" is to focus on simple accomplishments. This keeps me on track and helps me maintain. I learned this mental trick after my season 5 breakdown, when I was on the brink of leaving *Jersey Shore* for good. During the six days that I was home and trying to screw my head back on straight, my therapist suggested that I do one thing every day that would get me out of my head and that would make me feel I'd accomplished something positive. "Start small," he said. "Eat a healthy breakfast. Spend one hour at the gym. Every day set a new goal, and once you've accomplished it, feel *good* about it." He emphasized the importance of not only accomplishing what I set out for myself, but also giving myself props afterward for actually pulling it off.

So that's what I did. Every day I set a new goal. (One that was achievable. I set myself up for success.) On Monday, for example, I might give myself a goal of running four laps around the high school track, and on Tuesday, I'd challenge myself to beat that goal by running five. Every time I accomplished what I'd set out for myself to do, I'd make a point of giving myself credit for my accomplishment.

I'd mentally say something like *Good job, Vin,* or *I'm stronger than my anxiety. I am in control of making myself feel good. I can control the crazy.* The act of giving myself props minimized my anxiety and made me feel better. Not *all the way* better, but incrementally better. Every day, my anxiety started to feel a little less intense. Eventually I felt more good than bad, my confidence got a boost, and that's when I decided I could return to the Shore and finish out the season.

Remember—confidence is a life-changer. It puts *You* back in control. When you're feeling strong and confident, your critical ego has a hard time keeping you in a stranglehold.

### VINNY'S MENTAL WORKOUT

## Give Yourself Props

On a daily basis, set a new and achievable goal for yourself. This could be anything—getting out of your pajamas and dressing up in nice clothes, getting yourself out the door on time, completing a homework assignment a week before it's due, or working out fifteen minutes longer than you usually do at the gym.

Whatever it is, give yourself props for the big and small things you accomplish. This is an important mental workout to do—both when you're feeling shitty and beat up and as preventative maintenance. Give yourself props *before* you get into a negative place. When you do that, you might "go there" a lot less often.

For example, let's say you've just taken a test. You didn't totally kill it, but you're pretty sure you did well. Instead of focusing on the questions that caught you up and you didn't answer, focus on the ones you nailed. Say to yourself, *Look at what I just did. I accomplished something here.*

When I was feeling sad and mad scared throughout the first season of

*Jersey Shore,* I'd often focus on how shitty I felt when I was out in the clubs and how I wasn't acting like myself. Instead, I should have been saying, *Vinny, even with all of these sad, anxious feelings jacking you up, you're still going out. You're doing it! You're a beast!*

Focus on the positive, on what you've accomplished, and feel *good* about it. That sense of accomplishment will stick with you. It'll be in your back pocket, and when the next challenging situation pops up in your life, you can use that sense of accomplishment to give you the confidence you need to take on the challenge and kick ass.

When you take time to notice your positive accomplishments, you give your confidence a boost. This is another way to create that positive mind momentum I've been talking about. Remember, every negative thought has a positive counterpart. Switch tracks by noticing your accomplishments. This will give your mind the positive momentum it needs to beat down stress, worry, fear, frustration, or whatever negative feeling that's blocking your way.

---

Since joining *Jersey Shore,* my day-to-day life has become nonstop and pretty chaotic. I'm always on the go. When I'm not shooting, my day might start with a car picking me up at six in the morning to take me to a photo shoot in Manhattan that lasts eight to twelve hours. Or I could be flying from New York to Miami, then off to Los Angeles and back through Chicago, all within a week's time, to make club appearances where there will be a million girls screaming for me (I hope!). Or I could be on the road giving thirty interviews in a row to local and national TV and radio stations. You're thinking, *Wow, Vinny, high-class problems!* I know what I'm describing sounds pretty cool, and I admit, I'm the luckiest guy I know. I'm not complaining. Still, a celebrity lifestyle means I have to always be *on,* which means that at the end of the day, I must remember exactly who I am. To do this, I absolutely must maintain my program and do daily workouts to separate my combative ego from my chill, cool, and calm true self.

Is this a struggle? Absolutely. Life finds ways to test me all the time. While I've developed many tools to help me maintain my inner cool when I'm confronted by tough situations, I'm not immune. I'm not "cured." And I never will be. I often say, "Nobody is perfect. I am nobody." But perfection's not the goal or the point, anyway. Life is about how we tackle and deal with the challenges we're faced with. Remember, struggles and hard times are an inevitable part of life, and when one presents itself, it's an opportunity to swing back stronger than the last time. Battling the negative noise is a lifelong fight, but I, and now *you,* have the upper hand to win another round and stay in the ring.

# EPILOGUE

## ONE HUNDRED PERCENT

After my season 5 knockdown on *Jersey Shore,* when my anxiety snuck up from behind and hit me so hard I felt like the only way for me to get back up off the ground was to bail from the Seaside house for nearly a week (sometimes the only way to combat negativity is to remove yourself from a situation), I returned to the set and sat down with my roommates and shared with them the truth about my struggle.

I opened up to them, as I have done with you throughout the pages of this book. I told them that when pushed too hard, I can fall into a dark and scary place that feels very difficult, and sometimes impossible, to climb out of.

Revealing this about myself on camera was a big deal for me. I'd kept my "secret" pretty well hidden for four seasons. I'd faked my way through a lot of crazy pain because I didn't want to be labeled as the "weirdo," and then be criticized, made fun of, and hounded by the press. I fully admit, I was ashamed. I felt inadequate. Why couldn't I just "man up"? For most of my young adult life, I'd thought something was wrong with me and that my mind went to crazy places no one could relate to or understand. This feeling of inadequacy was a beast to bear, and as *Jersey Shore* developed and became more and more popular and high profile, the pressure to hide my anxiety reached unbearable proportions. There finally came a point during season 5 where I was, like, *Fuck it. I have this problem. It's not bullshit, and I'm not going to try to hide it anymore. This is who I am. Take it or leave it.*

I'd already started writing this book as a way to deal with my struggle head-on, so I knew the truth was going to come out eventually, and I figured—I'm on reality TV, and it doesn't get more *real* than this. So, in front of my seven roommates, along with my producers, several cameramen, the guys in the sound booth, and the random nineteen-year-old intern working as a production assistant, I confessed on camera—I suffer from anxiety.

Once I came clean, a couple of cool things happened. I felt massive relief, and also—no one freaked. In their own ways, each of my roommates let me know that I was okay and they weren't going to abandon me. After five dysfunctional seasons together, we'd all seen the worst of one another, so on a deep level, I guess I'd already known that I could be real with them. But it's still hard to bare it all, you know? Especially in front of people who've come to know and *expect* you to be a certain way—in my case, the drama-free, fun-loving Vinny who's "got it together." But here's the thing, as soon as you show the world that you *don't* have it all together, that you have a weakness or a vulnerability, you quickly realize you're not alone. Everyone's got their own shit. *Everybody.*

I struggle with anxiety. That's *my* thing. I don't know what yours is, but whatever *it* is, I hope I've given you the courage to be honest about it. I'm not saying you need to go as far as I have (getting all emotional and confessing to millions of people on national television that you're on the ledge, that you feel like you're losing your mind), but at the very least, be real with *yourself.* Whatever gets you down, makes you crazy mad, or holds you back from feeling really good about yourself and your life—own it. There's no sense trying to stuff that shit down. Trust me, it will rise to the surface. I've learned that there's no shame in admitting that life can be friggin' hard. Sometimes it can feel really bad. A lot of times, the challenges we face seem bigger than we are.

And yet . . .

What I've also discovered is that we each have the power to make our lives better in an instant. You have absolute power to control your crazy. You don't have to wait until a year from now, after you've spent hundreds of dollars in therapy, to feel better. (I'm not saying that therapy can't help. I've spent a lot of worthwhile hours on the couch.) Instead, you can take a shortcut and feel better about your life *right now.* For real, this very minute you can start to improve your life by simply changing how you think. By using the triple-threat mind-body-spirit tools I've shared with you, you can take back control of your feelings, actions, and reactions. Seriously, once you change your *mind,* everything in your life will start to change with it. As I've said before, this isn't always easy to do, but you can do it if you put some work into it. That's what I've done, and my life just keeps getting better, one hundred percent.

Your life is your business. I'm doing my thing. You do you. All I'm saying is that when you turn down the crazy, it's like waking up out of a bad dream. Once you shake off the dark cobwebs, rub your eyes, and take a look around, the world becomes better and brighter. No wonder—you've woken up to *You*.

# VINNY'S READING LIST

Rhonda Byrne, *The Secret.*

——, *The Secret: The Power.*

Deepak Chopra, *The Seven Spiritual Laws of Success: A Practical Guide to the Fulfillment of Your Dreams.*

——, *The Seven Spiritual Laws of Superheroes: Harnessing Our Power to Change the World.*

Wayne W. Dyer, *Getting into the Gap: Making Conscious Contact with God Through Meditation.*

——, *The Power of Intention.*

——, *The Shift: Taking Your Life from Ambition to Meaning.*

Thich Nhat Hanh, *Being Peace.*

——, *The Miracle of Mindfulness: An Introduction to the Practice of Meditation.*

——, *Peace Is Every Step: The Path of Mindfulness in Everyday Life.*

Paul Hedderman, ZenBitchSlap.com.

Napoleon Hill, *Think Rich and Grow Rich.*

Sakyong Mipham, *Running with the Mind of Meditation: Lessons for Training Body and Mind.*

M. Scott Peck, *The Road Less Traveled: A New Psychology of Love, Traditional Values and Spiritual Growth.*

Rebecca Rosen, *Spirited: Connect to the Guides All Around You.*

Miguel Ruiz, *The Four Agreements: A Practical Guide to Personal Freedom.*

Madisyn Taylor, *DailyOM: Inspirational Thoughts for a Happy, Healthy, and Fulfilling Day.*

Eckhart Tolle, *A New Earth: Awakening to Your Life's Purpose.*

———, *The Power of Now: A Guide to Spiritual Enlightenment.*

———, *Stillness Speaks.*

Neale Donald Walsch, *Conversations with God: An Uncommon Dialogue.*

# ACKNOWLEDGMENTS

I would like to take a moment to thank a few people who have helped this book go from a vision to a reality. First, I would like to express how grateful I am to my team at Generate, my management company, who spend time every day fighting for me, managing my life, and setting up my future. Kara Welker walked me through the entire process of finding a literary agent, going to pitch meetings, and handling the book "business." Through it all, she helped me to stay extra calm and collected. I would also like to thank Antranig Balian, Alex Gregor, Jared Hoffman, Chris Pollack, Dave Rath, Dave Tenzer, and everyone else at Generate who believed in me from the start and continues to help me build my career.

I'd also like to thank Yfat Reiss Gendell at Foundry Literary + Media. You're one of the most positive and professional women I've ever met. Thank you for listening to a "self-help" idea from a kid on a reality TV show about partying, and then pitching it to publishing houses that publish books by presidents, the Dalai Lama, big-time doctors, and spiritual gurus! Without your dedication and connections in the literary industry, this book probably wouldn't have been taken seriously. Thank you also to Stephanie Abou and the whole Foundry team for your help.

In addition to helping educate me about the book business, Yfat also introduced me to the woman who was with me every step, word, edit, and phone call of the way—my coauthor, Samantha Rose. Sam, we are two completely different people, yet I told you things that I've never shared with anyone, and you formulated it all into this kick-ass book. Thanks for being so cool and stepping out of your "hipster box" and creating this with me. It has truly been a joy to work with you.

I'd also like to thank my publishing team at Crown Archetype, especially my editor, Mary Choteborsky, for believing in this project and walking me through the process of creating an informative book that speaks to my audience. Also at Crown, I would like to thank publisher Tina Constable for taking the time to let me explain my vision to her while she was on vacation in the middle of the woods and then allowing this partnership to occur. Thanks also to director of publicity Tammy Blake and to senior publicist Ellen Folan, marketing director Meredith McGinnis, as well as to Amy Boorstein, Terry Deal, Lauren Dong, Luisa Francavilla, Michael Nagin, and Jennifer Reyes.

Moving on, I would like to thank my on-set therapist Dr. B, who got me through some of the toughest times of my life. Through his teachings, he literally pushed me up the steepest hill I have ever faced and taught me a lot of what I share throughout these pages. Seriously, I wouldn't even be on *Jersey Shore* if it weren't for him.

I want to thank my *Jersey Shore* production company, 495 Productions, especially SallyAnn Salsano and Pam LaLima for introducing me to Dr. B and letting me talk to him whenever I wanted while filming. It was tough opening up about my inner issues on national television, but I was always confident that both of you were looking out for my best interests. As it turns out, 495 and MTV have given me the platform to deliver my program to millions of people.

At MTV, I would like to thank Chris Linn, Jackie French, and Jessica Zalking for supporting and approving this book. It's always interesting telling you guys what new ventures I'm up to, and I was so glad to hear that you were on board with me writing this *kind* of book. MTV is a great network to be a part of. I always say, "I play for the Lakers," because MTV is so much more than a television network. It's a pro-social *institution* for young people. *MTV Act* specifically reaches out to youth in need of a helping hand.

Now I want to take the time to thank my personal friends and family who have helped me in every aspect of my life. Doug Paton, thank you for giving me my first self-help book, *The Power of Now,* and sharing your knowledge with me while you were going through your own pain. To my sisters, Antonella and Mariann, you are my rocks. You've gotten me through the worst times of my life. I feel as though I can tell you anything, and much of the advice you've given me has been folded into my program and included in this book. To my mom and dad, thank you for shaping me to be the man I am today. Sometimes we go through problems that cause us to resent our parents for raising us in a way that might cause us stress later on in life, but I believe that everything happens for a reason, and if I hadn't been anxious growing up, I never would have gained the knowledge that I'm able to share today.

To everyone I've thanked here, and also to those I'm sure I

missed—you are all good people who were brought into my life for a reason. People like you prove to me that we are all inherently good, giving people who are put on this Earth to help bring meaning to one another's lives. This is the point of *Control the Crazy*. I love you guys.

# ABOUT THE AUTHOR

Vinny Guadagnino was born and raised in Staten Island, New York, and comes from a traditional Italian American family.

Vinny is best known as the "drama-free voice of reason" on MTV's *Jersey Shore*.

Vinny graduated from CUNY College of Staten Island and was a political aide for a New York state assemblyman. He took the LSAT and planned to attend law school, but since *Jersey Shore*'s success, Vinny's professional interests have shifted from law to entertainment and acting. He has guest starred on MTV's scripted comedy series *The Hard Times of RJ Berger*, MTV2's *Guy Code*, and the CW's *90210*, and will appear in Syfy's feature-length movie *Jersey Shore Shark Attack* in 2012.

When he's not entertaining, Vinny focuses on pro-social issues. He's a spokesman for MTV's A Thin Line antibullying campaign and MTV's GYT: Get Yourself Tested campaign and is a regular commentator on *MTV Act*, a blog that highlights young people, celebrities, and organizations that take positive social action. Additionally, Vinny is a spokesman for the Jed Foundation, which works to prevent suicide and reduce emotional distress among college students. He's also affiliated with and lends support to the It Gets Better Project, GLAAD, and DoSomething.org.

Furthermore, Vinny is a social media juggernaut, with more than 2.5 million loyal Twitter followers and an active YouTube channel (VINNYGUADAGNINO).